D0857452

Ascending Flame,
Descending Dove

Ascending Flame, Descending Dove

AN ESSAY
ON CREATIVE TRANSCENDENCE

by Roger Hazelton

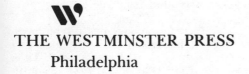

THE WESTMINSTER PRESS
Philadelphia

BOOK DESIGN BY DOROTHY ALDEN SMITH

Published by The Westminster Press®
Philadelphia, Pennsylvania

PRINTED IN THE UNITED STATES OF AMERICA

Grateful acknowledgment is made to the following for permission to use copyrighted material:

Harcourt Brace Jovanovich, Inc., for lines from "Little Gidding," in *Four Quartets*, copyright, 1943, by T. S. Eliot; copyright, 1971 by Esme Valerie Eliot.

Kayak, for a stanza from William S. Merwin, in *Animae*. Kayak, 1969.

The Christian Century Foundation, for portions of "Truth in Theology," by Roger Hazelton, in *The Christian Century*, June 23, 1971. Copyright, 1971.

Library of Congress Cataloging in Publication Data

Hazelton, Roger, 1909–
Ascending flame, descending dove.

Includes bibliographical references.
1. Transcendence (Philosophy) 2. Transcendence of God. I. Title.
BD362.H38   231'.7   75–9649
ISBN 0–664–24767–9

Contents

The dove descending breaks the air
With flame of incandescent terror.
Of which the tongues declare
The one discharge from sin and error.
The only hope, or else despair
    Lies in the choice of pyre or pyre—
    To be redeemed from fire by fire.

—T. S. Eliot

Preface

THE THEME that is sounded in this short book has concerned me for a rather long time. I have always been particularly attentive to those features of my own experience which could not be stated but only suggested, outside the range of my comprehension and competence, quite beyond the obvious and the ordinary. It therefore came as no surprise that transcendence has generally been a word to conjure with in Christian thought, although its meanings have been neither uniform nor fixed. Indeed, experiences of going-beyond and of being entered-from-beyond make up a considerable part of Christian faith itself.

Today, transcendence questions bulk large on theology's basic agenda. One also hears of "signals," "models," "myths" of transcendence in the arts and sciences. People of all sorts and conditions express a kind of hunger for the transcendent, whether by a deepening interest in the esoteric, occult, or ecstatic, or by efforts to raise the threshold of awareness through disciplines of group encounter, meditation, and chemical experiments. What does it mean that a transcendent dimension to human existence is so widely sought after and affirmed? How may theology in particular take the measure of these explorations?

I learned my theological craft from liberal thinkers who were chiefly engaged in making Christian faith intellectually acceptable to "modern" men and women—a task that seemed to leave little room for inquiry into the transcendent dimension. Much of liberalism's trust in reason and its practical optimism have long since left me, though I still maintain the conviction gained then that theology must always have the ring of humane truth regarding how things stand and go with us, what we have the right to expect and the duty to achieve in the world we know best. The liberal stress upon experience as the needed matrix of theological reflection has, I hope, been gratefully incorporated into my own teaching and writing.

However, I have had to carry on my vocation in a period of sharp reaction against liberal premises and methods. As everybody knows, there were good reasons for this recoil, both cultural and clinical in nature. The darker intimations of human frustration and finitude that liberalism had either overlooked or played down came back with a vengeance in neo-orthodoxy. Transcendence, it was then declared, belonged to God alone. The only help or hope for humankind lay in accepting Jesus Christ as God's ultimate will and final word, as revelation "direct from above," quite apart from human readiness or capacity to receive this revelation. But I could not accept the view that revelation creates its own response in human beings, or that it comes to us like a bolt from the blue out of somewhere "back of beyond." What I did learn and tried to teach was that one does not say God merely by saying man in a loud voice (Barth); and I found students and readers who were in no position to disagree.

Sooner or later these opposing insights had to come to grips with one another in my own thought, or at least to lie down together like the lion and the lamb in Isaiah's prophecy. The opportunity was provided by the present situation in theology. In certain respects a return to liberalism appears to be in progress. Theologians are generous in providing rationales for committed action on behalf of political, racial, or sexual liberation; the social context of theology is being carefully looked into; secular experience is being probed for meanings and values formerly reserved to the religious realm. Whatever is left of transcendence, it would seem, has been taken away from God and given back to "what man can make of man."

But in other respects the heritage of neo-orthodoxy is still strong, and the ferment it caused has by no means subsided. God remains "the problem," as John Courtney Murray, Gordon Kaufman, and others have kept reminding us. Can we actually rest content with what Dietrich Bonhoeffer called "this-worldly transcendence"? Would anyone have predicted, twenty or more years ago, that secular and radical, even atheistic theologies would have been put forward as the Christian truth for our time? Yet this is just what has occurred, and with a depth of impact in the theological community that is only beginning to be felt. The "death of God" motif, for example, which some prefer to dismiss as an outmoded fashion, has been growing in the modern consciousness for the past four centuries, and it will be a long time dying. What theologian can avoid coming to terms with this reading of the human situation, however he or she might wish to have it otherwise?

Speaking for myself—and this is what theologians tend to do at present—I confess that this vision of a world and of humanity without God both appalls and exhilarates my thought. On the one hand, I have lost all confidence in an objective superbeing, "the great white Christian in the sky," as a student once expressed it, who is believed to create, rule, judge, and save everything in history and nature. Evidence for such a superfact simply does not turn up in my experience or in that of my contemporaries. But on the other hand, I am dogged by the persistent suspicion—is this perhaps my faith?—that there is far more to the business of being and becoming human than the analysts, statisticians, and explainers have thus far produced. There are, I deeply believe, mysteries and wonders in our life that need acknowledgment and celebration after long neglect. For is it not, above all, in the sphere of symbol and of value, in the interplay of images with ideas, rather than by so-called facts, that our world's future is being formed? Are we not still open and available to the transcendent? If this is true, then new modes of sensibility and vulnerability toward one another and to the environing universe will be required for living in the age to come.

In short, I am committed to a "more-than" rather

than a "nothing-but" way of understanding what being human means. Neither scientific reductionism nor revelational positivism appears to tell the whole true story. Hence I resist being made to choose between "God" and "humanity" as if these were antithetical absolutes. The truth is actually more full and flexible. The key is given by a way of thinking of transcendence which is ancient yet new: we transcend ourselves by virtue of that which transcends us; our humanity is given us by that which is more than human, yet not other than human.

Therefore I am reluctant to abandon the word "God" at least until a better term has been found to indicate that reality in which we live and move and have our being. For the present, leaving names aside, it seems important to relocate transcendence in theology, as the following essay seeks to do. The title is symbolic of the human spirit's creative linkage with what has traditionally been termed the Holy Spirit. In this mysterious involvement of the intimate with the ultimate, I believe that there is a significant clue by which the sterile fragmentation and polarization in contemporary theology may be overcome.

It is pleasant to acknowledge the occasions that launched the writing of this book and to express my gratitude to persons who have encouraged its growth. In the fall semester of the academic year 1971–1972 I was invited to serve as visiting professor at the Pontifical Gregorian University in Rome, teaching a *cursus optionalis* in "Man and Transcendence." I wish to thank Dean René Latourelle, S.J., and Professor Jan Witte, S.J., of the faculty of theology for their most courteous hospitality. In April 1972 I gave the presidential address to the American Theological Society on the same topic; this paper was included in *Theological Studies* for December 1972, and portions of it are used here by permission of the editor, Father Walter Burghardt, S.J. An opportunity to deliver the Russell Lecture at Tufts University followed in October 1972; my host was Professor Howard E. Hunter, with whom I have had many friendly contacts in the Society for the Arts, Religion, and Contemporary Culture.

An invitation to give the Samuel Robinson Lectures at Wake Forest University in March 1973 enabled me to get the book into definite shape. This lectureship "to promote free and scholarly exposition of the Christian faith in its fullest meaning and application to the questing minds and human needs of the present age" is sponsored by the department of religion. To its chairman, Dr. E. Willard Hamrick, and his colleagues I express my heartfelt gratitude.

Portions of two articles have been reworked for publication here: "Symbolizing Transcendence," in the *Andover Newton Quarterly* for March 1974, and "Truth in Theology," in *The Christian Century* for June 23, 1971. This material is used again by permission.

I wish I might thank individually my students at Andover Newton, my colleagues in the Boston Theological Society, and other friends of long or recent standing, who have contributed to the making of this book. Two persons, however, deserve special mention. My longtime friend and trusted guide in theological matters, Daniel Day Williams, died in December 1973; the book intends to honor his memory. And as before, I thank my wife, Jean, for her constant interest and forbearance, even through the most enticing of summers on the coast of Maine.

R.H.

1

By Way of Introduction

LANGUAGE WATCHERS in our time have often noticed how words tend to lose their former liveliness and resonance. Alan Pryce-Jones, for example, after visiting the United States, remarked in the London *Times* Literary Supplement for May 19, 1972:

Words to the contemporary American are not supple, elusive things which conceal or divulge precise shades of meaning; they are not concepts to be loved and chosen, but, on the contrary, something like fill to a builder. They cover holes of thought; they offer a flat surface.

If all due allowance for British condescension is made, the comment is not without its point. Common speech today is pretty generally undistinguished by either spaciousness or color. Even the language of blame and praise favored by politicians, like that of customary reverence still used in religious circles, is noticeably lacking in sincerity and depth. Saddled with prefabricated, patched-up connotations, robbed of their primal, natural wonder, words all too often become flat surfaces that are grossly unsuited to the sharing of real thought.

This being so, anyone who deliberately tries to convey ideas by means of words is well advised to inquire just how this aim may be achieved. Such a project, if it is not to be a mere rehearsal of the obvious, will need to employ language of suggestive and exploratory power. The notion that all words exist on the same uniform level of meaning, that they simply indicate or refer to something dryly called "facts," must be stoutly avoided. There are dimensions of promise and surprise even in ordinary speech, all-but-hidden metaphors, indeed a whole firmament of symbol, which make our communication unmistakably human. Language is mysterious in both its origins and its objects, so that saying just what one means to say is neither easy nor simple.

Take, for instance, the phrase chosen to open up the range of meaning traversed in this book. "Creative transcendence" may evoke for some the thought of one more self-help program, or perhaps the slogan of a new religion based in Los Angeles or Tokyo. It is true that words such as these have lost much of their ancient amplitude; once they had something to do with God, but today they keep cropping up in lesser and more limited contexts. Nevertheless their histories render them capable of setting up reverberations and tensions for our deepest thought. They are certainly supple and elusive enough, at any rate, to provoke reflection on the matters with which this book is concerned.

I

Throughout the greater part of its history the word "transcendence" has been closely linked with the idea of God. It was a technical and not a popular term, used by theologians and philosophers whose chief interest was to distinguish the God idea from all other ideas. Although the word belonged more to the schoolroom than to the sanctuary, its very abstractness served to heighten and sharpen the meaning of God that is proper to confession, prayer, and adoration. Theory does, after all, have the function of guiding and refining practice; and "transcendence" is but a neater, more conceptual word for saying with religious faith itself that God's ways are not our ways nor his thoughts our thoughts. As a kind of sentinel or warning term, it stood guard over the ultimate otherness of God with respect to everything natural, rational, or only human.

By trying to preserve a necessary element of negation at the core of faith's own affirmation of God, the transcendence motif in religious thought served to protect faith from its most insidious enemy—that making and remaking of God into man's image which ancient prophets called idolatry and modern psychologists describe as projection. Worship requires a nonaccommodating, nonmanipulable other, precisely in order to be worship rather than a mode of self-congratulation. Popular religion is always tempted to forget this, whenever it ignores the built-in self-criticism which the idea of a transcendent God provides.

However, it should not be supposed that transcendence functioned in a solely negative, critical manner. One of the most instructive accounts of its use in Christian theology is given by G. L. Prestige, writing about the thought of the early Greek fathers. He comments:

The negative prefixes so widely employed in words intended to describe the divine nature really testify to divine freedom and independence. . . . His absolute independence is a corollary to his absolute goodness and wisdom, as well as to his absolute capacity to create. . . . Thus the emphasis on God being uncreated implies that he is the sole originator of all things that are, the source and ground of existence, and the conception is taken as a positive criterion of deity. . . . This by no means implies that God's relation with the world is one of Epicurean remoteness.[1]

Hence the stress upon divine transcendence, from the beginnings of theological reflection on matters of basic faith, has embraced both negative and positive meanings. The idea involved is not simple but complex: independence does not mean isolation, but fullness and wholeness of being; the nature of God as over and above the world is not indifference but signifies a superlative, incomparable abundance. So Prestige points out that in the thought of the church fathers God's incomprehensibility is associated with infinity—scarcely a purely negative attribute—and, commenting on Clement's statement that God is without anger and desire, shows that it means not the mere absence of passion but rather that God's will is "determined from within instead of being swayed from with-out" (p. 7).

Negative terms do not necessarily connote a lack or a denial of meaning; they may in fact be chosen to suggest an overabundance of meaning which can only be communicated by hesitancy and reserve. There are times when straightforward language used in positive description or definition does not suffice. During the ages of faith, when belief in the Biblical and Christian God was culturally powerful, this was notably true. Hence transcendence language developed in order to name the object of devotion without robbing the object of its singular, surpassing importance. Speech about God had to be "appropriately odd," in Ian Ramsey's phrase, precisely in order to be *about* God rather than some item in the experienced world. As Augustine put it, "If those who speak so much [about God] fall so far short, what of those who do not speak at all?"

To be sure, when God becomes more a matter of doubt than one of faith, a new and different situation has to be faced. Then, under the corrosive action of "the acids of modernity," the idea of God tends to lose its habitual specific, objective reference and may even become a candidate for oblivion. For the past four hundred years this process has been going on, signaling the eclipse of an ancient and honorable view of transcendence understood as God. Later in this book we shall address the question whether such an identification still makes sense in terms of our contemporary experience. Here, however, the point to be made is that for modern thinkers the transcendent is no longer limited to the divine. This shifting of the ground of meaning is a "fact of life" for persons and societies alike and must be accepted as such by both believers and nonbelievers. Indications of what has happened to the use of transcendence may be found in fields as diverse as philosophy, literature, and psychology. It was Immanuel Kant who employed the word "transcendental" to mean those factors which appear to regulate and organize our experience without themselves being items in that experience. For Kant, incidentally, God became a "postulate" useful chiefly in understanding the experience of moral claim and duty. Later, the term "transcendentalism" was adopted to describe the thought of Ralph Waldo Emerson and the group influenced by him; though here the word had already taken on the overtones of what traditional theology called divine immanence. And today, psychologists may speak of "self-transcendence" when they wish to examine the purposeful, normative, or ecstatic aspects of human behavior.

Two features of this development are especially noticeable. First, the meaning of transcendence is no longer confined to God but applies to human ways of being in the world. Second, the word has become more flexible both grammatically and logically; it may refer to experiences of transcending no less than of being transcended—that is, to an active rather than a passive or responsive kind of experience. This shift and broadening of the base of meaning is significant for what we are to be exploring in this book, but obviously there is much work of discriminating, sorting out of meanings to be done. Although we shall not be engaged solely in word study, the placing and weighting of key words cannot be avoided. It is only fictional characters like Humpty-Dumpty who can "pay words extra and make them mean what I like"; real people have to take words where and as they find them, and move on from there.

II

The word "creative" has a similar history. It also was used by religious thinkers to further differentiate God from everything that is not God. Primarily, of course, it called to mind the mighty act by which "the Maker and Father of all things" brought them into being. The result of this action was termed "the creation," thereby emphasizing what Søren Kierkegaard believed was "the infinite qualitative difference" between creature and Creator.

The thought behind this traditional usage may be abruptly summarized as follows. Nothing in the known or knowable world explains itself; questions can and should be asked regarding its causal connections with other things. It exists relatively, not absolutely, needing to be explained by something else, and finally by something that is not another "thing" at all but rather the transcendent will of God. Since only God has his reason for being within himself, everything else in all creation is originally and ultimately dependent on the divine independence for whatever existence it may have. This idea of God as the self-caused First Cause once again asserted God's utter freedom to be God by acting according to his own nature and will, apart from inner pressures or outward influences of any kind. God, then, is the reason why there is a world at all; one can start anywhere in the world and reason one's way back to its divine source and ground. This thought has persisted in many forms throughout the modern period; it fascinated a philosopher like Spinoza, served as the basis for Schleiermacher's analysis of religious experience, and was decisive in dislodging Thomas Merton from his youthful skepticism, to give but a few examples.

Nevertheless, the reserving of creative action to God alone is an idea that has lost much of its power over modern consciousness. Today it is human beings who are called creative; the word most often refers to the making of works of art. True, it has become so thoroughly secularized—and trivialized—that it may conjure up such things as fashion designing, television programming, or a scrumptious salad. The point, however, is that it no longer marks the traditional difference between God and man. In fact, for those of theological bent, creativeness itself signifies "no dualism of divine and extra-divine nature, of God's absolute transcendence of the world and of man. . . . Everything which happens with man happens with God."[2]

This changing of the base of meaning should be worth exploring. The usual explanation has been to the effect that religious ideas are in process of becoming secularized in our culture, so that old Nobodaddy, as William Blake ironically called God, has vanished from the stage of here and now where modern living must go on. Although one may regret or resist this situation, it must at all events be recognized for what it is, for there can be no turning back to the old assurances by which former ages lived.

Now this is true, but is it true enough? I believe that the cultural situation is marked by processes of secularization and by an attitude of mind predisposed toward secularism, and that there can be no point in denying this. However, the whole truth is far more complex. When attributes once reserved to God become clues for interpreting human beings to themselves, then significant changes take place in the way men and women understand and value their own capabilities. The loss of a commanding, workable idea of God may only serve to show that transcendence and creativity need to be relocated. It may mean that the God question and the humanity question are really one question. Perhaps the trouble lies in our attempt to keep these questions separate, even to polarize them, as if humanity and God were external to each other.

Studies in human creativeness, for example, indicate strongly that experiences of breakthrough into new insight—particularly in scientific fields—often cast considerable doubt upon the mechanistic or deterministic theories with which such work is carried on. Creativity is both receptive and constructive: willingness to be instructed by fact, nonresisting and open, is balanced by effortful, deliberate action taken to articulate and validate what has been discovered. These moments are fused in each instance of what Alfred North Whitehead called "the creative advance," and together give to it the qualities of *seeing* and of *making* that distinguish it from routine or repetitive behavior. The human virtues of freedom, courage, and daring, quite as much as those of humility and veracity, are brought into play.

Where do you suppose the idea of a creator-God came from, if not from such experiences of human creativity? It is not as if we first knew who God was and then interpreted what being human means according to that prior knowledge. It is not as if we somehow deduced that there must be a God from evidence supplied solely by human weakness or limitation, in order to compensate for our felt deficiencies. It is not as if we had to depend on faith in a far-off outsider-God to gain a proper view of human possibilities and resources; Berdyaev was surely right in saying that "truth about man can only be revealed by man himself."[3]

This, I take it, is the point of the contemporary stress in theology upon translating statements about God into statements concerning human life. This would be misunderstood if it were thought to be a simple replacement or reversal of one kind of language by another. What seems to be happening, rather, is that the whole God question is being reopened in the context of the nearer, more insistent question regarding the essential meaning of our humanness. The latter question is taking shape on many fronts and in many modes of anxious reflection, from the privacy of isolation to the public manifestation of growing indifference to basic human rights and values. If theology has no genuine contribution to make to this crucial inquiry, it deserves to be ignored and indeed abandoned.

III

Thus far the theme of this book has been introduced in standard, straightforward prose, which is the accepted—and expected—manner of discourse used in pressing home such matters. Why, then, has a curious compound image like "ascending flame, descending dove" been chosen to convey the thrust of the book's intention?

The truth is that we live more by symbol than by explicit statement of "what is the case." A later chapter will give further evidence and reasons for this truth, especially as it bears upon the expression of experiences of transcendence. Suffice it here to say that there is more than one level of human meaning and that some levels are more profoundly expressive than others. Even if I speak of "plain, unvarnished truth" or "brute fact," I am making use of ill-disguised images in a rather ironic effort to show that imagination has nothing to do with the case. And if I speak of human failure in terms of breakdown, or success in terms of adjustment, I am tacitly comparing persons to machines, as if such a comparison really meant something important. Every statement that can possi-

bly be made has its implicit basis in a symbolic net-
work, resting as it does upon assumed likenesses or
correspondences between one level of meaning and
another. It would seem the better part of wisdom to
acknowledge this instead of persisting in the somewhat self-defeating business of pretending that images
are irrelevant to the pursuit of what we please to call
the truth.

The compound image chosen to set forth the argument of this book is, it may be recognized, that employed in Christian thought to signify the Holy Spirit.
The doctrine of the Trinity has always regarded the
Spirit as one of God's ways of being God, coequal with
the Father and the Son. Yet the place of the Spirit
within the Godhead has never been fixed either theologically or liturgically. Father and Son are images of
personal relationship, but spirit is a curiously imper-
sonal idea, connoting rather a kind of capacity or energy or vital principle which is God in action. The
primitive root of the word maintains a marvelous ambiguity of meaning; spirit is associated with wind, an
external force that is felt but cannot be seen, and also
with breathing, which is the most inward sign of life in
conscious and unconscious organisms. The Spirit is
God because God is Spirit, invisible but powerful,
coming and going without fixed location in space or
time, and yet, in the words of Dante and of Augustine,
"the Life of our life."

Throughout the Jewish and the Christian Scrip-
tures, spirit is referred to as that invisible dynamic
reality linking divine with human being, that mysteri-

ous aliveness which makes possible not only contact but communion between them. It is not too much to say that spirit is here conceived as common to both God and humankind, not as a territory occupied by both but as the gift of one that constitutes the very being of the other. Human aspiration has its energizing source in divine inspiration; in the words of the Biblical proverb, "The spirit of man is the candle of the LORD." Human and divine being are, in the Roman Catholic term, "connatural," each participating in the reality proper to the other, but without losing the identity of either.

Christian interpretations of the Spirit of God are controlled by the overwhelming conviction that the divine has entered human life in Jesus of Nazareth. The Spirit has become Word and the Word has become flesh, that is, has taken up its abode in a finite, fragile being. This "great and mighty wonder" is most often symbolized in terms of a divine descent; Paul even calls it the self-humbling of God. Hence it is not out of keeping with this central symbol that at the baptism of Jesus the Holy Spirit should come down "in the form of a dove" to manifest the divine approval of the one chosen to carry forward the messianic mission.

The dove, ever since the ancient myth of Noah and the flood, had been the image of the cessation of hostilities between man and God, the harbinger of God's *Shalom* or reconciling peace. There could hardly be a more fitting figure of the Holy Spirit than this messenger bird, often chosen as a sacrificial offering in the

Temple worship. In Christian art the dove appears not only in depictions of the Trinity but also indicates more generally the incoming, indwelling power of the divine. Even in so-called secular painting, such as the still lifes of Georges Braque, filmy dovelike evocations of transcendent presence may be traced. Evidently this particular symbol has not lost all its suggestive value for contemporary experience.

Corresponding to the dove image of the Holy Spirit is the flame image of the human spirit. When God's Spirit "came upon the church" at Pentecost, according to the book of The Acts, the disciples present behaved with such joyous abandon that onlookers judged them "drunk with new wine." As an outward sign of their inward ecstasy, we are told, tongues of fire hovered above their heads. The appropriateness of this symbol consists in its fusion of the themes of surrender and of self-fulfillment: the flame both burns and illumines, consumes and completes our natural humanity. Frequently in descriptions of mystical experience the phenomenon of fire appears to body forth a similar feeling of burning, radiant intensity that lifts and enlightens. In a familiar Christian hymn the words "My heart an altar, and Thy love the flame" convey the same meaning.

There is at least one recent work of art in which these symbols of the flame and the dove stand together. It is an untitled painting by Jan Le Witt, dated 1973. Done in abstract expressionist style, against a pale-orange background, jagged and furry vertical brushstrokes create a zone of contrasting blackness edged in blue-gray. Within this dark portion appear the two symbols; the white bird wheeling and turning is on the right, and the flame, an oval reddish glow veined with blue, is to the left. The whole work possesses, for one viewer at any rate, a singular grasp of that courageous self-giving and self-fulfilling which in this book we call creative transcendence.

IV

Today it has become all but impossible to inquire candidly and sanely into any issue without taking sides. One wonders if there ever has been a time when part truths masqueraded as they do at present in the guise of the whole truth. Thus it becomes highly unlikely that any truth unfavorable to a previously held opinion can be seen or stated, except by someone already locked into the contrary opinion. In the arena of public discussion every situation quickly turns into an adversary situation, every issue is polarized into a pro and con format, and the ensuing conversation takes on the semblance of a secondary school debate. It is a sad time for men and women of goodwill who simply wish to know how matters stand, what has happened, and what decisions are to be made.

Unfortunately, contemporary theology has tended to fall into the same either/or trap. Here the lines seem to be drawn in an essentially political manner between conservatives and radicals, traditionalists and revisionists (who of course are *anti*traditional).

In particular, the view that a choice must somehow

be made between God and humanity as mutually exclusive objects of loyalty functions almost as a kind of dogma. This means that whatever truth exists on both sides cannot serve to correct and complete a common search for truth. But it is not the case that what the large words "God" and "humanity" stand for can be factored out into separate entities presumed to be in some sort of competition for the prize of truth. Do we not see now more plainly than before that the question about God is wholly bound up with the question about what being human means? And has it not become finally evident that when we ask what makes men and women truly human we are also raising the archetypal, universal question concerning what our fathers and forefathers knew as God?

The inherited distinction between the divine and the human has plainly lost its force. It was too heavily loaded with symbols that cannot honestly reflect contemporary questioning: symbols of monarchical authority, military conquest, patriarchal ownership, even male supremacy, and their servile opposites. There are good reasons why such symbols no longer work for us, religiously and otherwise. This is why the task of theology must always be done over again, in an attitude of flexibility tempered by fidelity.

Any tradition is a living and growing form of historical process. It may include elements of narrowing and hardening effect that invite resistance or revision. But to think of tradition as some kind of massive mistake whose weight must once and for all be gotten rid of is merely a gesture of immature impatience. There is a possibility of new insight that always lives within old interpretations of the truth, a possibility neglected or rejected at some earlier time, since the past consists as much of discarded possibilities as of actualized decisions.

Furthermore, a tradition as ancient and complex as the Christian heritage includes the seeds of its own renewal. When Paul wrote to the church at Rome on the subject of allegiance to Jewish traditions, he pointed out that the true descendants of Abraham are those who live by Abraham's faith in the promise made to him. Bloodlines, like ritual conformity or legal observance, are incapable of guaranteeing genuine loyalty to a heritage that consists chiefly of promise. The criterion is not repetition but participation. Indeed, the repeating of wonted formulas and actions may indicate the absence rather than the presence of inherited faith. Evidently it cannot be said too often that when faith is warped into propositions claiming certain truths, it ceases to be faith. The same thing must be said about habitual religious behavior, which may only represent a shaky insecurity and defensiveness. Robust participation in a living tradition is altogether compatible with willingness to keep ultimate questions open.

The Christian tradition, considered as a whole, maintains a notable balance between transcendence and immanence in speaking about God. Since both kinds of statement may be found in theological writings, it is rather easy to attend to one while ignoring the other. Then the balance must be redressed, perhaps taking the form of a strong counterstatement. After all, in propositional language only one thing can be said at a time. When we choose to speak in this fashion about God we are required to use one-thing-at-a-time linear language. To be sure, occasional reminders that this is not all, that there is more to be said, may help. But generally, in theology as elsewhere, truth comes in bits and pieces, and a long view is therefore indispensable, as well as that generous-mindedness which is often called humility.

Speaking theologically, the guiding principle to be followed in this book is that transcendence and immanence are mutually implied in any view of God that claims to be "Biblical" or "Christian." If the emphasis here falls most often upon immanence—that is, upon the indwelling and enabling character of God—that is because so much theology of the recent past has stressed unduly the divine transcendence, thereby endangering the sensitive balance that theological work must always seek to preserve. This fair and lucid comprehension may be more often honored in the breach than in the observance; nonetheless, it finds expression in a passage written by William Ernest Hocking more than sixty years ago:

In proportion as the religious horizon is drawn close, the gamut of religious experience becomes trivial. . . . The nearby deity of a religion that betones immanence proves in experience to be a baffling object of worship. Paradoxically enough he is not so accessible as the unreachable God. . . . The explanation of the paradox seems to be this: that the effort to think God must first differentiate God from our other objects. But *we also* are in a different world from any of our world-objects; something in us is foreign and transcendent to all that we view. . . . Until the human spirit knows the self that is more at home in the infinite than here among Things, it has not yet found its Self nor its God. Only a transcendent God can be truly immanent. This also is a matter of experience.[4]

By way of amplifying and updating Hocking's conviction, the ensuing chapters will be devoted to understanding the ways in which transcendence is experienced, thought about, symbolized, and lived. The question of God will linger on the hidden agenda, as it is bound to do in any serious approach to transcendence. But the main thrust of the book will be in the direction of what has already been termed here the humanity question. In a familiar Quaker metaphor, we shall be concerned to explore "the Beyond that is within."

2

Experiencing Transcendence

DO WE HAVE experiences of the transcendent? The question is not as simple as it looks. To be sure, it is a factual, not a logical question. That is, it is a matter for inquiry carried on by the methods appropriate to the human sciences. However, this does not mean that such an inquiry has no logic of its own, nor that logical rules are unimportant. Indeed, the way in which we define or conceive the transcendent may distort the very form of the factual question and may even inhibit the process of getting answers to it. So it is well to begin our inquiry by asking what its ground rules are to be.

I

The verb "transcend" originally signified in our language an act of crossing over or going beyond, action begun and completed by human effort. But since the act of transcending involved overcoming some obstacle in the transcender's way—a river or a mountain perhaps—the word also came to signify the barrier itself, that which "transcends" the would-be transcender. So by a kind of reversal, which is not uncommon in the history of language, transcendence came to mean a state or condition of being transcended. In ordinary use it may even mean what cannot be transcended. This change from active to passive voice has implications and reverberations far beyond the merely grammatical.

If transcendence is defined, either explicitly or implicitly, as what is inconceivable or unknowable, then obviously—by definition—we can never know or think it. If it is defined as impossible to experience, then no experience can be invoked as its expression or effect. In such instances, as H. G. Wood remarks, failure is not only invited but is assured.[5] Perhaps this is why so many current discussions of transcendence are logically caught on dead center. Or, to change the figure, they can never get off the ground because they have defined themselves in terms of an impossible task.

This impasse, however, is only a logical one. In fact, people will go on thinking and talking about transcendence, and they will doubtless continue to define it in the kind of language that suggests unthinkability and unspeakability. Does this indicate that perhaps we ought not take our definitions too woodenly or too solemnly but should change the rules when a new sort of game is in progress? Yes, I believe it does.

If I persist in defining the transcendent as what cannot be known or experienced at all, and then go on talking about it anyhow, there must be some good reasons for acting in so interesting a manner. At least I must have some dim and flickering understanding of what I think cannot be understood. Does not my knowledge of anything also include a knowledge of my ignorance about it, that is, of the gaps or limits that qualify my knowing? There is nothing utterly incredible or devastating about such a situation, although it may sound paradoxical when described in linear language. But it does seem that I am taking a long and rather gratuitous step when I call something unknowable just because it is unknown. If I am merely voicing the difficulty of the mental operations and word changes the situation requires, then my discomfort is real enough but it should not be projected onto what I am trying to understand.

It is a question of fact whether the transcendent can be or ever is experienced, but the answer may involve revising the idea of experience with which we began. Abraham Maslow's study of what he termed "peak experiences" provides an instructive example. The information he collected has undoubted psychological value, even though he insisted that it all could be given a completely naturalistic explanation. Maslow's inquiry suggests once again the residual, holding force of an earlier positivism and reductionism in the human sciences that may defeat its own empirical purposes. Yet his work had considerable value in freeing academic psychology from a monotonous leveling of human experience to subhuman behavior, even if it seemed to affirm and deny transcendence at the same time.

The researches into extrasensory perception carried on over the past several decades represent another kind of exploration into the factual question. They are mentioned here only to suggest that such inquiries are legitimate even if their conclusions should prove distinctly controversial. To ask the question of fact, using controlled situations and precise standards of observation, is surely indispensable for gaining present-day attention to any new understanding of transcendence.

Theologians too have engaged in an empirical attempt to specify the phenomena of transcending and of being transcended, quite apart from any argument for or against the existence of God, or at least before such an argument is advanced. Here belong the "models" of Gordon Kaufman, the "myths" of Herbert Richardson, the "signals" of Peter Berger, among others, representing new sorties into a very old terrain. These theologians, like many of their colleagues, are actually looking at human experience for indications of a range of reality that cannot be reduced or confined to experience. Whether it is their deliberate intention or not, they seem to be moving toward the abandonment of a contents-of-consciousness reading of experience which has long been plaguing modern discussions of transcendence.

This welcome and encouraging turn, or return, to experience charts a promising course for future thought. The work of John E. Smith has been particularly helpful in showing how consideration of experience in terms of its so-called contents greatly impoverishes our understanding of what any "fact of experience" is. The upshot of this view, writes Professor Smith, is a highly theoretical factualism and neutralism modeled on techniques employed in the natural sciences. It leads inevitably to the unproved assumption that experience consists in making "subjective" additions to the neutral facts. Someone —it may have been Professor Whitehead—has remarked that when a person says something is a matter of fact, you may know that he is at his wits' end. Knowledge is not a glassy eye beholding a ready-made reality, as John Dewey used to say. These are valid protests against the notion that factual knowledge as one kind of experience can legislate for all the rest of experience. There is no single set of standards that every candidate for credibility must meet. This does not mean that there are no standards but only that they must reflect the multidimensional and multidirectional nature of experience itself, which William James called "booming, buzzing confusion."[6]

The question whether or not the transcendent is experienced may be complicated, but it is also unavoidable and momentous. In any case, transcendence seems to be a constant background or accompaniment to all experience, whether its dominant tonality is scientific or dramatic, cognitive or affective, factual or imaginative. I transcend and I am transcended; I even transcend myself, whenever I think and know myself thinking or act and feel myself acting. I have no way of getting outside my own skin, although I am quite aware, in Michael Novak's words, that I am not "an ego in a bag of skin."

II

The part played by transcendence in experience can be detected in various ways. One traditional route has been by the study of religious behavior, beliefs, or symbols. That way is still open, but there may be real difficulties in thus narrowing our attention. Hence a better starting point at this particular cultural juncture may be provided by attending to the artistic experience. There is today a more general acceptance of the values and meanings associated with works of art than with those regarded as explicitly religious. And this is to be expected, as the necessity of fashioning a more humane future for our world has become a paramount concern in which the arts have a decisive stake. If the role to be played by religion is much less assured, there is at all events a committed vanguard of people who have been discovering a common ground of action and reflection with creative artists. That ground is the zone of the truly human as contrasted with the standardized, pressurized travesties that smirk and posture everywhere. Already it has moved well beyond common brooding over what Rico Lebrun called "the unmanageable design of our condition" toward collaborative efforts to create visions and incentives capable of changing that design for the better.

Thomas Merton's lifework is an eloquent example of this contemporary movement. He was acutely conscious of intimations of transcendence existing outside the religious institutions that formerly regarded the transcendent as their prerogative. He wrote:

I had learned from my own father that it was almost blasphemy to regard the function of art as merely to reproduce some kind of sensible pleasure or, at best, to stir up the emotions to transitory thrill. I had always understood that art was contemplation, and that it involved the action of the highest faculties. . . . I had understood that the artistic experience, at its highest, was actually a natural analogue of the mystical experience. It produced a kind of intuitive perception of reality through . . . effective identification with the object contemplated.[7]

It may well be true that artistic modes of experience are marked by an immediate and whole acquaintance, a direct participation, not different in quality from the vision of God so prized in earlier generations.

All art is visual in the sense that it intends to see and make seen. Vision, indeed, is probably the oldest and most universal metaphor meaning every kind of knowledge or understanding. But such a metaphor, in saying what it means, does not mean simply what it says. When, for instance, the Bible speaks of "the eyes of the heart" it is not referring to cardiac optics but to "perception lifted to the pitch of passion," in Henry James's words. To see, in any but the most literal sense of the word, is always to intuit, to imagine, to mean more than is said. For metaphor is the stuff of which a fully human world is made. Unless we live by symbol, song, and story we do not live at all; we merely vegetate or react, and these too are metaphors for a nonmetaphorical existence. Our very bodies serve as metaphors in which, by a transfer or carry-over of meaning, we express what takes place in "the mind's eye" of imagination. Metaphor, indeed, may be one of the principal means by which human beings "hold body and soul together"—that is, insist upon giving expression to our humanity.

The stress here laid upon vision through metaphor is necessary because many persons today seem caught in the grip of a dreary factualism that is inimical to human growth in every sphere. Literal exactitude, not amplitude, tends to become the sole norm of learning and knowing. We grow uneasy in the presence of anything but the barest statement of what is the case. But men and women are not data processors and there are other kinds of precision than those practiced in the analytical sciences. Do we not therefore need to begin all over again by reclaiming our imaginative birthright? Surely it is chiefly by exposure to works of art that this endowment may be restored and nourished after long neglect. For art, says Herbert Read, "is really a vital activity, an energy of the senses that must continually convert the dead rain of matter into the radiant images of life."[8]

The sort of vision encouraged by the artistic imagination is no mere looking or staring. Authentic art confronts us with both a surface and a depth of meaning. The surface arrests our attention, magnetizes it so to speak, while the depth insinuates itself by turning regard toward reflection. What is being said in art is that something more is meant than what is said. So, viewing the intriguing canvases of Joan Miró, the sheer playfulness of those swirls and squiggles in their tantalizing space becomes "eye-opening." Or one may read William Blake's poem about catching butterflies and happiness:

> He who bends to himself a joy
> Does the wingèd life destroy;
> But he who kisses the joy as it flies
> Lives in eternity's sunrise.

Saying one thing to mean another is characteristic of all creative art. There is more than appears on its surface and yet the surface is where the depth begins to appear. Does this amount only to a sort of double vision in which meanings get imposed upon matters of fact? Hardly. The creative process and its product are profoundly one. Blake's short poem, for instance, can be analyzed on paper into perceptual and conceptual ingredients, into a rather simple image on the one hand and a bit of moral advice on the other. But such a procedure necessarily violates the integrity of the poem as written and read, blandly ignoring its metaphorical fusion of sensuous surface with humane depth.

"We murder to dissect," as Wordsworth wrote. For the artist, the world is visibly, meaningfully one. A star or a butterfly may "speak volumes." Music and mathematics inhabit the same universe. In the arts, the so-called solid "world" of nameable, located objects and the so-called subjective "world" of fugitive impressions are *seen* to coalesce and coincide. Jungian psychologists interpret this process as being reawakened from the secondary and divided realm of consciousness into the primary, undivided realm of archetype and symbol witnessed to by the "collective unconscious." Whether we adopt their special vocabulary or not, the point is that in works of art barriers become horizons. As Henry David Thoreau put it, "Our present senses are but rudiments of what they are destined to become"; and art exists to see and make seen "a nature behind the ordinary" which arrests and beckons us.

Not all practicing artists would agree with this statement, of course. "You see what you see," said a painter recently, referring to the hiatus that must always exist between the work that is made and the work that is seen. Our aesthetic perceptions are notoriously variable and refuse to be "programmed." Nevertheless, as Albert Camus put it, "If the world were clear, art would not exist." That sight should become insight, across the boundaries of time and taste, is the implicit, if not always explicit, *raison d'être* of works of art. Cézanne once said about Claude Monet, "He is only an eye," then quickly added, "but what an eye!" Monet's paintings of Rouen cathedral done under different conditions of light and weather give special emphasis to that remark.

Artistic vision (*aisthesis*, "sense perception") is a theme with many variations, to be sure. Each work of art achieves or attempts it in its own particular way. Two examples from contemporary literature come to mind. A writer well known in France, Roger Martin du Gard, describes in a letter to a friend the difficulties of growing old. His eyesight was failing, he said, his work had gone sour, his colleagues and companions were dying one by one. What was left for him to do or to be? He wrote, "I am building myself a tiny cottage in the roaring forest of the world." Retelling the story of Orpheus, the American poet Denise Levertov mentions Orpheus' exile and separation from his beloved Eurydice, followed by his cruel dismemberment; but then in the poet's words, "his head still sang and was swept out to sea singing." Symbols like these illuminate the stubborn creativity of men and women beset and all but done in by adversity. They suggest the presence of a more-than-human humanness able to make music out of necessity. They weave a web of resolute meaning that arises from what has been called "the strange pride in being visited by a catastrophe."

III

Such glimpses of creative self-transcendence afford considerable insight into the felt texture of experience, to which and from which the arts of today speak. With their help we become questions to ourselves, as Augustine put it long ago. Indeed a virtual preoccupation with human identity typifies contemporary culture and the arts that give expressive, significant shape to it. Barnett Newman, who died recently, summed up the purpose of his lifework by saying, "The self, terrible and constant, is for me the subject matter of painting and sculpture." A century earlier Victor Hugo had observed that "the dark mirror is deep down in man." True, no artist, regardless of his or her gift for keen self-perception, can ever reduce the self to visual, verbal, or auditory form; yet this unaccomplishable task continues to fascinate and even to dominate artistic effort.

The preoccupation with one's own identity may easily turn into an obsession. In a culture that proceeds on its way generally indifferent toward artistic endeavor, the artist may be forced to raise the pitch of self-expression simply in order to be noticed. Nevertheless, this effort to give meaningful shape to the self, the person, belongs to the very grain of human creativeness. It is most of all in learning what one has to do that one discovers his or her identity, even when self-discovery as such is not the cause but the effect of creative enterprise. Moreover, a search for selfhood is no private or selfish matter, since it must be finally either accepted or rejected by others. Erich Neumann, writing from the Jungian viewpoint, emphasizes this:

One of the fundamental facts of creative existence is that it produces something objectively significant for culture, but that at the same time these achievements always represent subjective phases of an individual development . . . what emerges in the creative work is not only individual but also archetypal, a part of the unitary reality that is enduring and imperishable, since in it the real, the psychic, and the spiritual are still one.[9]

It is not necessary to adopt the theory of archetypes and the collective unconscious, much less the subject-object way of thinking, to agree with the truth in Neumann's statement of the matter.

One thing, at all events, is beyond academic dispute: creativity, if and when it appears, belongs to the sphere of human selfhood. It is persons who are creative. The course of what is termed the creative process may be charted by the use of various psychological or philosophical devices, but when all is said we are left with the mysterious and inexhaustible region of selfhood. The time-worn clichés of the schools cannot do justice to its clamorous reality, and it sits grinning at our vain attempts to capture it in some supposedly definitive phrase.

This is what is meant by self-transcendence as the term is used today for probing and evaluating human experience. In psychology, as analysis and therapy have been jarred out of previous maps of the self, a more spacious and sensitive understanding comes surely into view. Clearly, to be a self is to be more than oneself, not at rest but in motion, on one's way to a fuller and deeper self, however haltingly or ineffectively. As William S. Merwin writes:

> I am never all of me
> unto myself . . .
> Maybe I will come
> to where I am one
> and find
> I have been waiting there . . .[10]

Artists in search of themselves give voice and visibility to built-in human capacities for reliving, extending, evaluating experience. Their works of creative imagination reveal something of great importance not only for understanding art but every manifestation of human activity. They speak to and for all humankind. Genuine creativity is present only in the self-transcending self. It makes beginnings out of apparent endings, virtues out of necessities, and so recovers the original meaning of the word "transcendence" as a "crossing over," a "going beyond," a "passing through."

Virginia Woolf was a consummate artist who told stories to make this meaning clear. Once, commenting on Perugino's paintings in comparision with her own writing, she had this to say:

[I] achieve a symmetry by means of infinite discords, showing all the traces of the mind's passage through the world; achieve in the end, some kind of whole made of shimmering fragments; to me this seems the natural process, the flight of the mind.[11]

There is no reason to suppose that this self-understanding is more authentic than that reached by other, less "artistic" persons; it is only more conscious and articulate.

There is a real point in the saying that the artist is not a special kind of person but every person is a special kind of artist. A patient who is subject to chronic anxiety is engaged in examining and shaping the self, with a therapist's help, looking to a new level of insight and integrity. An oppressed minority moves from nonviolent resistance toward outright confrontation with the powers that be, committed desperately, yet with determination, to goals of freedom and dignity for all its members. These are not different essentially from the activity that uses stone, paint, or language to achieve "dynamic form" out of the tension set up by the interplay of psychic with material forces, resulting in a new creation. All give instances of the truth that to be a man or a woman means to be a self-transcending self with visions of possibility as yet unrealized but realizable.

IV

There is in progress at the present time a reconsideration of the interrelationship between the aesthetic and the religious modes of experience. During the past two centuries it was rather generally assumed that these modes could be sharply distinguished with respect to their objectives, feeling tones, and effects on human behavior. But one has second thoughts when a deeply religious thinker such as Jonathan Edwards declares that loving God and loving beauty come together in "true virtue" which is a "consent to Being-in-general," or when a painter like Georges Rouault breaks with the secular presuppositions of his art and finds his own vocation in returning to Christian themes. Then it is strongly suggested that to distinguish is not to divide, that there is unity as well as diversity between these forms of experience.

As Nietzsche wrote, "Gray cold eyes do not know the worth of things." What binds art and religion most closely together is the fact that both are rooted in experiences of passionate involvement and of ultimate commitment—in short, what F. David Martin in his carefully wrought book *Art and the Religious Experience* calls "the participative experience." Martin understands this type of experience as one to be contrasted with the spectator type which only skims the surface of what is presented, sitting in judgment and remaining outside what is taken to be its object.[12] Waiving for the moment the question as to whether this distinction is as definite or decisive as Martin thinks it is, it may surely be agreed that the differences are significant, even if only a matter of degree. One may either give oneself into the keeping of what is presented, or withhold that gift by maintaining "psychic distance" from it. But the participative experience seeks communion or identification, as far as possible, intentionally avoiding any judgmental, independent stance. And this experience is common to both religious and aesthetic concerns.

It is, of course, true that much talk today about being involved (which is what gears do when they mesh) misses the mark because it is so undiscriminating. Such talk expresses more of a protest against the "gray cold eyes" approach to truth and value learned in the schools than it testifies to a genuine self-surrendering participation. Nevertheless there is a real and palpable difference between "knowing about" and "being acquainted with," as William James used to point out; and this difference is germane for understanding every sort of experience. Furthermore, while

a moment of looking or attending, more or less pro-
longed, is necessary for entering into any truly participative experience, such a moment may and should
be followed by others of deepening insight and what
D. H. Lawrence called "insideness."

Aesthetic and religious types of experience are
more easily distinguished at their superficial rather
than at their profound levels. When seen in depth,
both are marked by a liberating openness to the solici-
tations of a reality that encompasses and expands
one's conscious self; both foster a sensibility that is
intimate and ultimate; and both are concerned "to
abide with Being," as Heidegger wrote, "to be at
home in the homeland."

Therefore it is eminently right to emphasize the
aesthetic element in the religious experience, as Jonathan Edwards did, since without such an element religion would be no more than a parody of itself. It
would lack every convincing sign of its own experiential authenticity. It would be all shell and no Spirit. As
Amos Wilder states in the introduction to his recent
book of poems, "Before the message there must be
the vision, before the sermon the hymn, before the
prose the poem."[13] The roots of motivation are firmly
intertwined with those of the creative imagination.
Just as decisive changes in a culture are first signaled
in its works of art, so those within the person often
spring from half-buried, half-forgotten images
grasped by the lower—and more open—regions of
aesthetic sensibility. It is correct to call every kind of
creativeness artistic in this sense, whether it is

predominantly religious or scientific, active or contemplative. But the bond between creative art and creative faith is singularly close because each is participative in high degree and embraces concerns identified with the other.

In the words of Berdyaev, there is a sainthood of daring no less than one of obedience. It may be added that the creativity proper to religious and artistic experience alike has common sources of affectivity and intentionality; between wonder and awe, between symbol and sacrament, there are significant linkages to be recognized. "I imagined that I bore my chalice safely through a throng of foes," wrote James Joyce, hinting with just a touch of irony at a priestly understanding of his art. And there was Rainer Maria Rilke with his "Angels," those guardians of the portal of his poetic inspiration.

Indeed, is there not "a nagging sense of the numinous" in works of art that last and speak beyond the time of their own making? Such a quality is necessarily more implicit than explicit, as it pertains to style rather than to subject matter. One thinks of pictures of Christ that have nothing numinous about them; they are religious only by convention, like postcards or medals purchased in a curio shop. But when Paul Gauguin, an artist uncommitted to any church or faith, paints Christ, he conveys a sense of the numinous or sacred by expressing his own work and life as a participation in Christ's suffering and sacrifice. Or consider the fantastic yet foreboding canvases of Paul Klee, emerging from what he himself termed "the secret place . . .

where the secret key to all lies guarded." Here are further indications that the artist keeps some sort of rendezvous with the numinous horizon celebrated at the most authoritative levels of religious experience.

In his influential treatment of the major arts in relation to religious forms of meaning, Gerardus Van der Leeuw answers affirmatively the question, "Can art be a holy act?" Although he is working with an idea of the holy too narrowly defined as "wholly other" and with an outmoded aesthetics of "the beautiful" that would win little support today, he rightly understands this question to be raised by the integral nature of human experience itself. "Our time," he writes, "is full of yearning for the lost unity of life. . . . Art participates in all of life, and all of life participates in it. . . . The artist makes the depths of things resound."[14]

V

The striking phenomenon called inspiration, since it is shared by religious and aesthetic consciousness, deserves a specific comment. Here once again we have a term that has had long and intimate associations with religious experience but is now utilized to interpret the creative process in the arts. This shift in the focus of the word's meaning, however, does not represent a total secularizing of the experience it designates. The mystery of transcending and being transcended belongs to both the older and the newer meaning. Inspiration, then, affords a highly pertinent vantage point for understanding how transcendence is experienced.

Biblical instances of inspiration are rich and varied. The most familiar are those mentioned in the prophetic writings. Here the Spirit of God comes upon or catches up the prophet, enabling the person so engaged to speak and act in extraordinary ways. This influx of power from the divine source may even be resisted by the prophet, although ineffectually. Inspiration is always involuntary in the sense that it comes whether it is sought or not, and is not subject to the prophet's own control. Yet at the same time it connotes a heightening and greatening of one's personal capacities, a summoning from beyond that is also a strengthening from within the self. Inspiration is a phenomenon of prophetic experience that intricately balances passive and receptive modes of consciousness, on the one hand, with active and creative modes, on the other. The prophet like Jeremiah who does not want to be one nevertheless becomes one. Saul, who though a king is a quite ordinary man, is singled out to carry forward the design of God for his people. Paul the apostle, blinded by his vision on the Damascus road, yet sees far more clearly than his sighted companions what is happening and what is to be done.

Prophetic inspiration remains a mystery to itself even after it has become integrated into the prophet's mission and vocation. Paul expressed this in the words "I, yet not I." The Spirit is no alien intruder into the human spirit, although the Spirit can never be domesticated there. There are well-intentioned but misguided Christian believers who adopt the word "inspiration" to guarantee the inerrancy of Scripture itself, as if certainty could be made out of mystery. But we have no warrant, either in faith or in reason, for substituting so-called inspired words for the persons who spoke them, or a text for the experience it attempts to communicate.

Can it be otherwise with the inspiration associated with authentic art? Here too the signs are eloquent in testifying to the communion of spirit with Spirit. The language used in describing artistic inspiration is seldom Biblical, to be sure. Even Jacques Maritain, no stranger to theological terms, chooses his words with care in the following statement: "Unexpressed significance, unexpressed meanings, more or less unconsciously putting pressure on the mind, play an important part in esthetic feeling and the perception of beauty."[15] It is at least a fair and open question whether "unconscious pressure" may not have undoubted affinity with what prior generations would have called "being touched by the Spirit"; and the question is merely foreclosed, not settled, by dividing up the whole of experience into compartments marked "art" and "religion." The only real issue lies between a "nothing-but" and a "more-than" reading of our experienced humanness. Either experience is curved in upon itself, bordered and limited by what is not itself, and therefore must be understood as reducible to basically subhuman factors and determinants; or experience is "absolutely open upwards," in Karl Rahner's words, to visions and energies that enter creatively into its very texture and substance. It is one of the main convictions giving rise to this book that art and faith, viewed experientially, stand together and reinforce each other on the "more-than" side of such an issue.

Throughout our history in the West, "more-than-human" agencies or "pressures" have been invoked to account for the phenomenon of religious and artistic creativity. Gods and muses throng the pages of ancient myths. Oracles and omens, visions and visitations come to men or women from these sources of spiritual power. The temple of Apollo at Delphi, the inner monitor, or *daimōn*, of Socrates, the wrestling of Jacob with the angel at the ford of the Jabbok, all belong to a pattern of interpretation in which experience is viewed as possessing the possibilities of transcending and of being transcended. The spectrum of inspiration ranges all the way from Dionysiac frenzy to Friedrich Nietzsche saying, "I never had a choice."

The fact that many instances of what was formerly called inspiration can be better explained by natural causes is hardly open to doubt. Nor is it to be denied that some of these experiences, or others very like them, may be chemically induced or else experimentally controlled. Such facts, however, do not make necessary the dismissal of every claim that inspiration has occurred, although they are of help in sorting out these claims more carefully. An experience may be accurately explained without being adequately understood. A cause-effect mentality has only limited resources for probing the intensities and immensities of experience. It is an error to suppose that the "How" of any human event is equivalent to the "Why" of that event. Keeping considerations like these in mind, the matter of inspiration is not easily disposed of, any more than it can be quickly settled in the affirmative.

Nevertheless experiences of being grasped and held by powers beyond a self's control or purpose do happen. Not all are favorable to one's growth and fulfillment; some may even be destructive and "demonic." As Christian thinkers have always said, not every spirit is the Holy Spirit; we must "test the spirits" to see whether they are "of God." Yet no logical rule, no laboratory situation, can provide such a test, since the evidence in question is elusive and indeed inexhaustible. The best way to decide is by considering "the fruits of the Spirit": do these claimed experiences of inspiration actually yield insight, encouragement, renewal for the self and others? Are they creative and re-creative in their effects? Do they contribute to a more humane and liberating order of life?

To be genuinely inspired means to become aware of resources for laying hold on what has been traditionally known as "newness of life." It is not surprising that inspiration should be associated with near-madness, since it stands in sharp contrast with ordinary, "normal" modes of consciousness and conduct. Psychologists have shown, however, that so-called madness may be in closer touch with reality than is a type of behavior dominated by habitual and quasi-mechanical attitudes. Fantasy is more germane to inspiration than an overriding concern with feasibility, adopting Harvey Cox's antithesis. Not normalcy but some degree of ecstasy is characteristic of our inspired and inspiring moments.

Could anything, then, be more humanly important than to call attention to those experiences of being taken "out of ourselves" by which transcendence becomes a matter of our deepest, truest selfhood? Pascal was right in saying, "Man is not made but for infinity," echoing the Biblical word of promise, "It does not yet appear what we shall be."

VI

Experiences of transcendence are not all experiences of creativeness. Some appear to have negative qualities from the viewpoint of the person undergoing them; they foster feelings of limitation, not of liberation. Twentieth-century existentialist philosophers have described many of these states with sympathy and precision. Terms such as "alienation," "finitude," "anxiety" have even become clinically useful in reading the human evidence. The picture that emerges from this literature is one of life being lived under conditions of appalling loneliness and frustration, yes, of exposure to a Nothingness with all the classical marks of nameless dread. Here transcendence means the presence of an aching, ominous absence of meaning, at least in any self-enlarging or creative sense. It must be regarded by human beings as encroaching upon and inhibiting their search for either identity or integrity.

But all of this could have been predicted from the hardening of myth into dogma, of mystery into sheer miracle, that has occurred in Christianity over at least the past seven centuries. When transcendence is denominated as God ruling the world from beyond the world, so that any instance of experiencing transcendence must be thought to be an intrusion from a wholly other realm of being and of meaning, then if transcendence should put in an appearance, it will be viewed as an utter miracle to be understood only in terms of absolute paradox. And when the grounds for believing in such an intrusive, alien reality begin to wither away, it is inevitable that the vacuum should be filled by Nothingness itself, rather than by Being in its plenitude and power. That is, of course, to say that the vacuum is not removed at all, but only accentuated and rendered as absolute spiritual zero.

It is inevitable that my experiences of the transcendent should raise questions and suggest answers regarding the ultimate meaning, or lack of meaning, of my life in the world. But they do not in themselves possess coercive force and are therefore open to more than one kind of interpretation. May it not then be true that a real ambivalence toward the transcendent is an essential feature of these very experiences? Must not our expression of them be authentic only when it is also ambiguous, capable of being taken in at least two very different ways?

"The deepest use of the vocabulary of transcendence," writes G. H. Woods, "is to describe the fact of being in existence."[16] The user of such language is not trying to describe something hidden behind what appears to him; nor is he—or she—giving names to a distinct sensible quality of objects, persons, or events. Transcendence is not to be located and pinned down so easily. Rather, it is the pervasive accompaniment of every genuinely human experience, whether of fear or gratitude, of loyalty or mistrust. Perhaps the word "mystery" sets forth as well as any other this experiential dimension or horizon. But since its usual current meaning is almost entirely negative, if not threatening, the word "presence" may be preferable. A character in one of Paul Claudel's plays goes so far as to confess, "What I do not understand I consider a personal insult." Whether insulting or not, the experience of presence-mystery is deeply characteristic of our humanness. It is the acknowledgment, however mute, of being other than my own, including my presence to myself in being.

If words such as "presence" and "mystery" seem imprecise, that is because the human situation requires that they be "supple and elusive." That is, they should reflect the hazardous yet fortunate ambiguity of our existence. Such terms do not belong in a discussion of the behavior of rats in mazes, but have their rightful place in trying to understand the contours and contents of distinctively human experience. They harbor possibilities of meaning that range all the way between plight and promise, frustration and fulfillment. They do not foreclose ultimate issues but disclose and join these issues.

Much more might be said about mystery and presence. For example, Gabriel Marcel devoted many pages of his work in drama, music, and philosophy to exploring their meanings in and for experience. Thus, describing presence as a "being-with" and not a simple "being-there," he proceeds to make its meaning clearer by an illustration:

It should be noted at once that the distinction between presence and absence is not at all the same as that between attention and distraction. The most attentive and the most conscientious listener may give me the impression of not being present; he gives me nothing, he cannot make room for me in himself. . . . The truth is that there is a way of listening which is a way of giving, and another way of listening which is a way of refusing, of refusing *oneself*. . . . For the one I am a presence; for the other I am an object.[17]

And as for mystery, which may be thought of as the underside of presence, there are in recent and current writing indications as compelling as they are diverse: Karl Jaspers' "the Encompassing," David Martin's "Inexhaustibility," Tillich's "Being-itself," Heidegger's "homecoming," to name but a few. The ground swell of this movement in contemporary thinking away from quasi-mechanical models for human experience is unmistakable; and not only philosophers and theologians but scientists and artists are participating in it more and more fully.

The reassertion in our time of the right of experience to be heard and heeded reopens the whole question of transcendence. There is a precious suggestion of this new yet also very old perspective in a saying of the Venerable Bede: "The life of man is like the flight of a bird." The bird flies out of the darkness through an open window into a lighted room, where it remains for a time, then it darts back through the open window into the darkness again. Is this a symbol of experience or of transcendence? Obviously, of both together. In an appropriately odd way it locates experience within transcendence, yet also relates transcendence to experience. Where we come from we do not know, nor where we are to go; but in this lighted space called the world we fashion our tokens of origin and destiny.[18] By means of symbols such as this, men and women experience themselves as transcending and being transcended, creating and re-creating a truly human world.

3

Symbolizing Transcendence

I

NOT MANY YEARS AGO, when I was living for a time in the ancient Japanese city of Kyoto, I became familiar with some Zen Buddhist writings. They often describe a dialogue between a student and a teacher, as in this example:

STUDENT: "If the Buddha is more than Siddhartha Gotama, who lived many centuries ago, then tell me, please, what is the real nature of Buddha?"

TEACHER: "The blossoming branch of a plum tree."

STUDENT: "What I asked, worthy sir, and what I am eager to know is, What is the Buddha?"

TEACHER: "A pink fish with golden fins swimming idly through the blue sea."

STUDENT: "Will not your reverence tell me what the Buddha is?"

TEACHER: "The full moon, cold and silent in the night sky, turning the dark meadow to silver."[19]

That is the dialogue reported in its entirety. We are

not told whether the student went to the bursar's office to get his tuition money back. Is this any way to treat an eager learner?

But suppose the Zen master, for all his seeming evasiveness, really wanted to show his pupil that he had asked an unanswerable sort of question. The nature of the Buddha is not a neutral, public fact to be defined in commonsense terms. Quite the contrary; it has to do with the kind of blessed reality that is open only to an alert, deeply personal responsiveness. So a student would do better to begin by attending more closely and feelingly to the rich detail and amazing variety of the world disclosed in his own experience, real or imagined. Plum blossoms, idling fish, or a cold full moon are more than data to be ticked off and filed away under abstract categories. They are, or may become, eye-openers that sharpen one's awareness of a livelier, larger reality beneath the surfaces of things. Then looking becomes seeing, and seeing becomes believing.

To us of the Cartesian, Aristotelian West the Zen teacher's replies sound exasperatingly irrelevant. They do, however, make a most important point. The sensuous world is not what Marcel calls "a desert of objects" but has a strange symbolic potency and vibrancy. Anything grasped in its singular, felt wholeness, as a presence in its own right, may convey a more embracing ultimacy of meaning. That it is capable of doing so is as much a part of the truth about it as its strictly visual and measurable aspects. In the words of Marc Oraison, "But the limits of science do not mark the limits of experience. No question disappears merely because we do not know the answer to it."[20]

Now people have always had to live with unanswered questions. Lived experience is not to be reduced to scientific specifications. We would be less than human if we did not, like the Zen disciple, ask about what exceeds exact knowledge or, like the master, give hints of answers by means of symbols that body forth what cannot be explained or proved. Symbolizing transcendence is an action as inevitable as it is strange; we have no other way to cope, yet cope we must.

In our particular epoch it is not surprising that symbolic communication as practiced by the arts and the humanities should be regarded with suspicion. Minds attuned to the requirements of exact science are not at home in the region of symbol. By what right or virtue does one thing come to stand for another, greater thing? Cannot every symbol be translated into the language of plain fact? Is there not a prose equivalent for every poem, a psychological explanation of every myth, a literal reading of every story? Whatever cannot thus be reduced to scientific terms must be relegated to the fantastic or the palpably absurd. As methods improve and data multiply, symbols may be expected to yield to facts.

A "nothing-but" cast of mind goes so far as to construct entire theories of symbolism on a supposedly scientific basis. Common to them all is the view that symbols are blanks to be filled in, ciphers to be decoded into a clearer language. As far as possible, they should be desymbolized into nonproblematic factuality. Then they will stop baffling and exasperating us.

Nevertheless, human beings cannot live for very long with such a "nothing-but" understanding of what is happening to them. The notion of a nonsymbolic world of mere objects is the oddest of all myths. It generates a sense of false security which is the antithesis of genuinely scientific tentativeness. We would not be men and women if we did not inquire about the nature of Buddha, about our own selfhood, about justice and freedom, beginnings and endings, all of which exceed the limits of our science. That is because transcendence is a vital element in all experience, making it both questionable and questioning, as science itself reveals. More attention should be paid to the creative, imaginative character of scientific work; it too is a distinctly human enterprise in which the making and use of symbols has a crucial role. A superstitious scientism is the enemy and not the ally of true science.

Therefore the issue is clearly drawn between a "nothing-but" and a "more-than" view of what is involved in symbolizing the transcendent. The alternatives are basically these: either our experience is itself symbolic, suggestive and expressive of reality, or experience is reducible to so-called facts which are the only reality with which we have to do. It should not be a difficult choice, although it is surely a momentous one.

II

A large body of writing has grown up around the subject of symbols and their uses. Since the word "symbol" is itself symbolic, matters can soon get very intricate and confusing. Most writers on symbolism, however, lean toward one or the other of the basic alternatives just mentioned. As one picks one's way through the literature, it is helpful to remember Robert Frost's observation that there is a book side to everything: there are no bare facts, no uninterpreted events in our experience. But it is also salutary to recall Alfred Korzybski's maxim that the map is not the territory, the word is not the thing. The truth embraces both accents and requires both.

There is an important difference to be noted between signs and symbols. A sign may serve as a kind of proxy or stand-in for what it signifies. The mercury level in a thermometer, numbers on the dial of a clock, a traffic light, a cross on the church steeple, are signs that have this referring or pointing function. So too are words, for language is a vast web of signs, some directly indicating their nonverbal counterparts, others implying further signs within a communicative context. A sign may be informative, like pointer readings taken in a laboratory; or predictive, like the ups and downs of barometric pressure; or imperative, like flashing red lights or a policeman's whistle. It may be more social-conventional or more organic-natural in its mode of reference, and often it is both. What all signs have in common is the function of referring to something other than themselves.

Taking one thing to mean another is behavior characteristic of all sentient life, from Pavlov's famous dog to poetic metaphor and musical rhythm. Here is a fairly commonplace example from the field of language: English speech has, or had, a convention that "pansies" means "thoughts"; this came about because the more fanciful French gave the name of *pensée* to the flower, and the English took it from there. Add to this their difficulty of pronouncing French words properly, and the convention is established.

It is rather easy to regard a symbol as merely a special kind of sign, for it too leads or points beyond itself to something else. Indeed, this is what all "nothing-but" theories of symbolism do assume. They tend to view all symbolizing in basically physical terms, as if they could be understood without taking into account their fully human dimensions. But how does a symbol signify? Not simply by denoting a corresponding object or event, but by being part of that which it is used to mean. In other words, the meaning of a symbol is bound up with its being so that to have the one is to have the other, to lose the one is to lose the other. The sun is a symbol of life-giving radiance because that is what it does. The cross is a symbol of suffering love because that is where it happened. It is not as if we could read off or factor out these meanings, then discard the symbols that serve to convey them. Although not identical with their meanings, symbols are inseparable from them. They have a life of their own, even though no symbol lives forever.

Paul Tillich described the symbol as participating in that to which it points. A plainer definition is given by Dorothy Sayers: "A thing really existing, which by its own nature represents some greater thing of which it is itself an instance."[21] It follows that symbols can be taken seriously on condition that they are not taken literally. They body forth what they designate and so cannot be traded for non-symbols without being deformed and devitalized. It is then far from obvious that a symbol, though it signifies, is nothing but a sign.

In the words of Paul Ricoeur, symbols conceal a "double intentionality"—if you like, a double meaning—that constitutes their "inexhaustible depth."[22] They can be said to vibrate with a kind of tension that arises from the fact that they both are and are not what they mean. If they are spoken or written—and sooner or later they will find their way into the universe of discourse—they will say what they mean by meaning more than they can say. This tension in the symbol makes it emphatically different from any sign. True, a sign may come to take on some symbolic qualities, and a symbol may deteriorate into a mere sign. Mutations of this sort are always taking place in human communication. Nevertheless, sign and symbol are noticeably different ways of meaning, and their differences are not to be disregarded.

Symbol is the flesh and blood of really human experience, not merely a means for communicating that experience. Through it the absent is made present, the whole is mirrored in its parts, the extraordinary is suggested by the ordinary. It fixes upon something perceived, or at least perceivable, as meaning something else that is not the object of perception itself. And it does this not by pointing at a distance but by "throwing together," as the very word "symbol" suggests, two levels of meaning otherwise unattached and incompatible. All language is woven of such a symbolic texture, consisting of one layer of meaning opening to another fresher, more inclusive layer; thus language keeps in fragile yet sure touch with its own "inexhaustible depth."

For too long it has been thought that symbolic meaning could be analyzed according to the subject-object format of modern science and philosophy. Hence the old tired debates about where the beauty of a rose or a painting is to be located: Is it "in" the flower or the canvas or "in" the viewer's eye? The little word "in" concealed a lot of mischief because it seemed so simple and literal, whereas it was actually symbolic. The image of containment settled nothing, because it was based on what Whitehead called "the fallacy of simple location." This fallacy insisted that symbolic meaning must be desymbolized into either neutral objectivity or felt subjectivity. Since the real world was supposed to consist of physically observable facts and their interconnections, what could not be located there should be relegated to the inferior status of unreal fictions. This whole process was influenced greatly by an inveterate distrust of human imagination which had operated in Western philosophy and science from their beginnings in ancient Greece.

We know today that these grandiose divisions will not work. Old Newtonian, Cartesian, and Aristotelian dualisms have spent their philosophical force. No longer is it taken for granted that speech and thought can "cut reality at the joints," as Plato hoped; gone are the days when it could be assumed that parts of speech conform to entities within an "outside" world. Gone too, for the most part, is the view that this "real" world can be properly described as consisting of static elements in physical space connected by cause-effect relationships that are measurable and predictable. In short, philosophers have been disabused of all such dreams of cosmic conquest; they are now content to analyze the forms and uses of language, to explore modes of human existing, or to describe recurring structures of awareness and activity. Most significantly, there is abroad in present-day philosophy and science a growing persuasion that "experience is metaphysical," in the words of Hocking. Hence it becomes far more interesting to probe realms of meaning than to define characteristics of external objects. Clearly, this involves new and sustained attention to symbols and signs of every kind.

Against this changing background fresh and often surprising realignments are occurring. However, the old contention between "nothing-but" and "more-than" readings of the symbol still remains. It is as if the medieval debates between nominalists and realists had been resumed, with the noteworthy difference that it is now the nominalists who call themselves realists. They appear to share the curious modern prejudice which believes that to explain something is to explain it away. By a kind of alchemy in reverse, symbolic gold is transmuted into baser elements—that is to say, into models, signals or other non-symbols which may well be anti-symbols.

To be sure, any credible view of the symbol is obliged to account for its physical and sensuous character no less than its suggestive possibilities. A symbol is concrete and specific, anchored firmly in the facts of bodily existence. It can be recognized and made effective only by virtue of its capacity for fusing the particular and the universal in a single experience. But, of course, this is not what nothing-but theorists intend to say. No wonder that Paul Tillich used to dissent when he heard the phrase "merely symbolic," as he rightly regarded symbols themselves as a kind of protest against the mereness in experience. There is nothing "mere" about any symbol; its meaning value cannot be dismissed by using labels such as compensation, sublimation, or illusion. This is true even of those "steno-symbols," as Philip Wheelwright terms them, by which we locate and orient ourselves in a demanding environment.

Every symbol, then, is a token of transcendence by which mystery is made present to experience.

III

Let us return momentarily to the Zen master and his not too apt disciple. Imagine them standing on a moon-viewing platform, perhaps at Nijo Castle or Kat-

sura Villa, watching the cold full luminary as it bathes
the surrounding gardens in silver. The teacher is saying in effect, "The Buddha is like that; this is his nature, too." By transposing the moon image into a
more literal language—and this is essential to an understanding of its meaning—we might construct a series of analogies or similes: The moon illuminates
mundane realities, transfigures them, places them in a
different light; the Buddha, in a way that is somehow
comparable, brings transfiguring insight where before
there was a confused dark.

Every transcendence symbol assumes a similar op-
erating base of meaning, more like a ratio or proportion than a common ground, from which a positive
comparison may be made. The moon is one of the
most familiar symbols of this kind. The fact that as-
tronauts have visited the moon, taken pictures of its
craters, and brought back samples of its surface has
led some literalists to suppose that its poetic possibilities are now exhausted. Nothing could be farther from
the truth. So long as humankind feels any sort of kin-
ship with the natural order, this symbol will continue
to exert evocative and expressive force. Remembering
the barren landscape pictured on a television screen,
poets of the future may find Masefield's description of
the moon as "a ghostly galleon tossed upon cloudy
seas" a bit too fanciful for their taste. But since the
moon, whatever it is made of, remains a visible part of
our experience, there is no reason why it should not
continue to be available for symbolic purposes.

Not only proportion but also perspective is provided by symbols of transcendence. They convey both likeness and unlikeness. The moon both is and is not a part of the scene over which it presides. It reveals earthly things in an unearthly light coming from a distant source. Thus a certain tension between the symbol and the transcendent is included in the symbol itself. It becomes a disclaimer making way for a disclosure. The symbol's adequacy depends upon an implied sense of inadequacy; it must say that it means more than it can say.

In the firmament of symbol, a straight line is not necessarily the shortest distance between two points. Gaps and detours belong to this realm no less than straightforward statement of what is the case. Something has to be left to the imagination, as the saying goes. Does this imply that transcendence should be allowed to speak for itself? Almost but not quite, since the creation of symbolic breakthroughs is itself a work of artistic skill. One must be brought to stand before an open door if one is going to look through it. What Denis de Rougemont calls "a trap for meditation" must be set before it can be sprung. If it is true, and it is, that the letter kills but the spirit gives life, then it is up to the spirit to find ways of uttering this truth in the various languages of art.

Symbols are not only possible but necessary for the sharing of experience which is permeated with transcendence. Instead of hovering at the very edge of experience, rather like a fogbank crouching just off an ocean shore, transcendence is experienced intimately and indubitably. One example is the relationship of a self to its body. Suppose, writes Whitehead, that you have lost your way and come upon a totally unfamiliar scene. You ask, "Where am I?" But you know that as usual you are "in" your body. What you ought to ask, says Whitehead, is instead, "Where are all the other things?" Here are mystery and presence with a vengeance. The relationship between myself and my body is far from clear, as it is one of the most elemental and pervasive instances of transcendence. The body gives me my identity, but I am not altogether identical with it. Is it my ally or my enemy, my instrument or my prison? It is all these things and more. Shall I say that I am my body or that I have a body? Both statements are true, however contradictory they may seem to be. The efforts of philosophers to make a problem out of this particular mystery have not been conspicuously helpful. It refuses to be literalized or behaviorized and will always break out of any formula that may be offered to explain it.

The human act called "knowing" is another instance of symbolic transcendence. To be sure, the processes of knowing can be analyzed indefinitely. By a series of reductions, intelligence can be given a cerebral, then a cortical, and finally a neural location. A lively academic debate at present centers in the question, "Is the brain like a computer or the computer like a brain?" Words like "circuitry" and "coding" figure prominently in the discussion, thereby providing yet another illustration of nothing-but versus more-than approaches to human issues. The question that is raised but left unanswered in this debate has to do with the *knownness* of what is known. Is something known until I know that I know it? Must not every act of knowing be reflexive in this sense? Michael Polanyi makes an important distinction in his writings between "from-knowledge" and "at-knowledge"; this, he notes, is the same difference that exists between "a person who, when reading a written sentence, sees its meaning and another person who, being ignorant of the language, sees only the writing."[23] Polanyi himself uses the word "transcendence" to describe this situation. Cognition is, at bottom, the recognition of a double transcendence that makes knowing both necessary and possible. As knower, I transcend what I know, and as something known, it transcends me.

Consider, further, the kind of transcendence that is disclosed in moral matters. What makes a human action "right" or "good"? Without entering here into the give-and-take of ethical theories, we can say that surely one factor in the rightness of an act is that the act is freely chosen, which means that it might have been otherwise. Choice is not to be confused with chance. It means decision, which in turn means selecting one possible alternative course of action among others that are also open or available. Old-fashioned philosophical determinists like B. F. Skinner deny this, of course; but if human beings are entirely controlled by forces in their behavioral environment, how can we say with Skinner that "man as we know him, for better or worse, is what man has made of man"?[24] One can

scarcely have it both ways and expect to be taken seriously. At the same time one can and ought to recog-
nize the truth in various positions—ethical relativism,
objectivism, and subjectivism; normative ethics, situa-
tional ethics, and the rest. It is difficult to see, however, that any fruitful ethical discussion may be carried
on without assuming "freedom to choose and to do
what is chosen," as Jonathan Edwards put it. This
again introduces the theme of transcendence.

Still another feature of experienced transcendence,
in addition to those of otherness and openness, is that
of oneness. When thought is engaged in thinking
about itself, it becomes truly reflective in the precise
sense of that word. That is, thinking about thinking
involves attending to what we think with, namely, the
methods and motivations that structure every thinking
act. And one of these is the unproved, unprovable and
yet undoubted and finally undoubtable persuasion
that thought itself discloses clues or hints of some
ultimate unifying wholeness. There are approxima-
tions to this persuasion that reality is not at cross-
purposes with itself in everyday expressions such as
"on the whole," "for the most part," "in the long
run." It is as if we could not finally believe in the bits
and pieces of truth that turn up without having some
sort of "whole idea" at the back of our minds—an idea
not clear and distinct, to be sure, but implicit in all
genuinely thoughtful activity.

Similar corroborations of "transcendence as experienced" might be adduced from play, work, dream,
love, or worship. A more-than-human quality informs

each mode and moment of our humanness. Transcending and being transcended belong to the very texture of existence as we know and live it.

IV

Symbols not only communicate the familiar strangeness of experience; they constitute its felt reality. Their meanings are not extraneous but are integral to its multidimensional suggestiveness. In John Donne's words, the purpose of symbol is that of "contracting the immensities" by bouncing one sort of meaning off another. Men and women do this kind of communicating; seagulls don't.

But now a further question, as we say symbolically, arises. Is there perhaps a sense in which the transcendent can be thought to symbolize itself? Before the idea is dismissed utterly, let its prominence in our own cultural tradition be recalled. Biblical language provides ample documentation: The heavens "declare" the glory of God, and the firmament "shows" his handiwork; day unto day "utters" speech, and night unto night "shows" knowledge. Evidently the Hebrew mind was captivated, not to say saturated, with this "show and tell" conception of natural happenings and objects. Transcendence in its most absolute form employs the furniture of earth and the choirs of heaven to bear witness to itself, sometimes graciously, sometimes terribly, always awesomely. Gerard Manley Hopkins, writing that "the world is charged with the grandeur of God," speaks out of the same tradition.

In the Christian West, sacramental symbolism rein-
forces natural symbolism. Actually, it fuses nature with
history, creation, and covenant in a most striking manner. A sacrament embraces both material and spiritual
levels of meaning in a single act. Divine self-disclosure
is conveyed through human activity. Reflection on the
symbolic potencies of water, bread, or wine yields the
conviction that they serve as "means of grace" enabling and invigorating and fulfilling life. A sense of
the holy embraces the commonest, most "secular"
happenings like cleansing and eating and drinking.
Sacredness is attached, not to the strange and distant
reaches of our experience, but to its most familiar and
intimate moments. Since the Word has become flesh,
it is the Christian vocation to effect a transmutation of
flesh into the Word. In sacramental action, this double
transmutation is believed to occur.

According to the mainstream of Christian thought,
a sacrament is "an outward and visible sign of an inward and spiritual grace." What this means is that the
transcendent, here named as God, manifests and even
materializes itself "in, with, and under" the sacramental elements. It is this gracious signifying action that
elicits the human response of faith. A sacrament,
therefore, not only is evidence of the way men and
women feel about God but also and primarily gives
witness to the way God is disposed toward humankind.
It represents—that is, makes present again—the prior
intention and initiative of God for us and our salvation. This is its genius, its *raison d'être*.

Such pledges or emblems of transcendent regard

and favor do not enter human consciousness as a bolt from the blue. They occur within a whole context of symbolic words, gestures, artifacts, persons, that give form to the sacramental experience. They participate in a sacramental universe. They do not domesticate or manipulate the transcendent, but put us at its disposal, calling its mystery by name and hallowing in that name the whole of human, natural existence.

The various arts of Christendom have contributed mightily to this deep sense of transcendence moving in and through our life in the world. Not only did they provide illustration for the gospel and give instruction in the faith; they sharpened human sensibility for the transcendent and set forth earthly life in a more than earthly light. They served to establish a perspective in which human beings could see themselves as they were seen by the God of grace and glory. In other words, Christian art embodied and encouraged a symbolic interpretation of existence marked by fundamental alternatives fraught with ultimate consequences. A tiny door carved standing partly open on a stone sarcophagus, sheep gamboling respectfully in a mosaic heaven, a Byzantine black Madonna staring wide-eyed from a side chapel afforded glimpses of this elemental awe and pathos in the presence of the transcendent.

The life of Everyman thus symbolized was indeed fragile and precarious. Being "absolutely open upwards" to fulfilling visitations from the transcendent, it was nevertheless also vulnerable to provocations from dark, destructive powers equally transcendent.

The angel was the symbol of the former, the demon of the latter. Somewhere between these opposing forces Everyman, blessed by one and beset by the other, had to find and make his way. Humanity was free, but free to choose and be chosen, for either weal or woe in the eternal scale of things.

Today everyone knows how shrunken and eroded this "holy fear" before the ways of life and death has become. Mysteries are downgraded into problems. Dragons and giants no longer stride the human world. Angels are legendary fancies relegated to an outgrown past. What good are such symbols when there is nothing left for them to symbolize? Nature stands mute; no longer a She but an It, the environing earth has ceased to speak what George Berkeley, as late as the eighteenth century, could call "a divine visual language" or to give forth what Jonathan Edwards thought were "images and shadows of divine things." The idea that transcendent will or wisdom is expressed in thunderstorm or harvest, in the tides of war and peace, or in the "music of the spheres" strikes most of us as simply preposterous.

And yet, if it is true that symbols participate in the greater reality they signify, the possibility of symbolizing transcendence must somehow be left open. Old symbols die and new ones take their place, but this may only mean that some kind of symbolizing will always be necessary. Do we not perhaps still entertain angels unawares? Is there not something of real value to be learned from those psychologists who now find "the demonic" a useful category for describing human obsessions of a virulent kind? It may be that at least some of the old symbols are not as dead as we supposed. May it not also be that newer symbols only do better what older ones have lost the power of doing—namely, that of enabling us to understand our experiences of transcendence breaking through and so encompassing our normal, all-too-human ways of feeling, knowing, thinking, acting? Surely the persistence and continuity of transcendence symbols requires more than a nothing-but interpretation.

From the contemporary study of language have already come important insights into how transcendence may be thought to express itself. The philosopher Martin Heidegger, for instance, describes speech as a capacity that is *given* to human beings; in his later view it is truer to say "The word speaks man" than to say "Man speaks the word." We are *languaged* by nature, since through our bodies we participate in its long and incredibly complicated evolutionary development. Indeed, a full understanding of the act of speaking or writing would require attention to a vast collection of physical, physiological, and psychological data, not to mention the fields of phonetics, semantics, and aesthetics. No wonder that Benjamin Lee Whorf declares:

Speech is the best show man puts on. It is his own "act" on the stage of evolution, in which he comes before the cosmic backdrop and "does his stuff." But we suspect the watching Gods perceive that the order in which his amazing set of tricks builds up to a great climax has been stolen—from the Universe![25]

In still another way, language is expressive of transcendence. As it incorporates the past, so it creatively prepares for the future. "Speech is not its own fulfilment," writes Hans Urs von Balthasar, "it is itself a beginning of action, and goes beyond itself in its involvement with life and its activities. The time comes when speaking is not enough."[26] It is as if language could only be itself by trying to outdo itself. Straining against its limits, language almost seems to take leave of itself by opening up a future in which speaking is not enough. Thus when Rainer Maria Rilke sought to put in poetic form the very purpose of his poetry, he wrote simply, "You must change your life."

Human discourse, like all symbolic communication, not merely specifies but exemplifies the transcendent. This is more clearly true of poetic than it is of propositional or systematic language, which is probably why Heidegger has moved in his own work from the latter to the former. His deepening interest in "essential" or "meditative" thinking as opposed to "calculative" thinking is reflected in the allusive richness and often baffling density of his own later writing. Such language can easily be criticized as deficient in the usual, expected marks of philosophical precision; but it must be judged by its intention, which is to fashion a mode of discourse that evokes the depth dimension of transcendent Being by suggesting its own contours disclosed by experience. The very failure of this kind of discourse is its triumph, for it can only succeed in its intent by becoming serviceable to the meanings that move through it.

For what do symbols actually symbolize? Obviously, they tell us much about ourselves that can be told in no better way. They can be read, and rightly, as indices of all-too-human fear or love, anxiety or courage. Yet no one who has really seen the Taj Mahal would be content to say that it is nothing but a prince's monument to his beloved wife, though it is also that. The contrapuntal harmonies of a Bach fugue, we believe, must have been stolen from the universe. Perhaps we should not get too mystical too soon about all this; nevertheless, a truly creative symbol has an urgency and vibrancy that will not be denied. It is more than a net of words or paint or music in which we propose to capture the transcendent and make it work for us. What it really does is to get under our rational guard, shatter our prosaic defenses, by allowing transcendence its own voice and shape.

Three centuries ago a Quaker writer, Isaac Penington, said with exquisite plainness something on this subject that we still ought to hear:

All truth is shadow except the last truth. But all truth is substance in its own place, though it be but shadow in another place. And the shadow is a true shadow, as the substance is a true substance.[27]

V

The final portion of this chapter is intended to provide a transition to the next, concluding chapter on transcendence in theology. What are the consequences of the line of thought sketched here for understanding theological work?

First, consider how deliberately symbolical the enterprise of theology is. Such an acknowledgment is especially useful at a time like ours when theology is widely conceived and practiced as analysis and argument bent on getting rid of the confusion that symbols always generate. One influential present-day theologian, John Macquarrie, does not hesitate to adopt the term "symbolic theology" for describing the work of interpreting doctrines based upon God's revelation given in Jesus Christ. In this respect, of course, Macquarrie simply repeats the classical Christian understanding of the creeds of the church as "symbols of faith." But he declares that once a symbol is understood "as a symbol," it may be discussed and illumined "in an alternative interpretative language" which makes all the difference between myth and theology. We who live in what Macquarrie calls a "post-mythical world" are called upon to translate inherited symbols into another kind of language, namely, one that is linear and propositional rather than imaginative and evocative.[28]

Macquarrie's view of symbolic theology is open to criticism on several serious grounds. Mythmaking and storytelling, in religion as elsewhere, have more to do with dream, play, or fantasy than with the literal explanation of events and objects. Hovering in the background of Macquarrie's viewpoint seems to be the old primitivist theory, now largely discredited by anthropologists, that people who live by myths always take their symbols literally, as if myths were a poor substitute for science. The truth of the matter is hardly that simple. Men and women in every age, not least our own, live by myths that give transcendent meaning to their experiences. True, the style and structure of these myths is neither uniform nor constant, despite astonishing symbolic repetitions and recurrences. As Pascal wrote, "We only change our fancies."

Patterning his thought on that of the early Heidegger, Macquarrie insists that Christian symbols must be validated by "the language of being and existence" which he regards as more universally communicable than the symbols themselves. This move from symbolic to conceptual meaning, from concrete expressiveness to logical abstraction, is what Macquarrie believes theology intends and carries through. To be sure, he does grant that faith symbols have "an intrinsic and illuminating connection with what they symbolize," and further that "perhaps in the interpretation of symbols we can never do more than illumine one set of symbols by another set."[29] Here, as in numerous other instances of his use of the little word "perhaps," we are left in considerable doubt regarding Macquarrie's principle for working with, rather than from or around, the whole symbolic texture of the Christian faith.

Would it not be preferable to state ungrudgingly that theology is symbolic in a more substantial sense? This must be so, since "all truth is shadow except the last truth." Theology, more than most kinds of inquiry into humanly significant truth, has what may be termed a high symbolic content. Image, metaphor, paradox, analogy, remain indispensable means for conveying theological meaning. A Christian symbol such as the Trinity represents an achievement of the faithful imagination. The theologian's task with respect to it is that of keeping the symbol truly symbolic while trying at the same time to say what it "really means." The fact that a whole body of doctrine has grown up around the symbol indicates that it is not devoid of conceptual, logical content; "Father," "Son," and "Spirit" have usually been identified by abstract qualities such as "unbegottenness," "begottenness," and "procession," or "power," "wisdom," "love." More recently, the Trinity has been reinterpreted in ways that disregard its symbolic form; so Cyril Richardson views it as an attempt to harmonize absolute and relational aspects of God—an effort he judges, not surprisingly, to have been a theological failure. And Paul Tillich in his exposition of the doctrine contended that it has nothing to do with the number three, thereby betraying his unwillingness to take its symbolic form seriously. However, three-in-oneness is essential to the meaning of the doctrine; and the lesson to be learned from such manhandling of the trinitarian symbol is that it cannot be made to mean whatever one thinks it ought to mean. Its recognized power to magnetize Christian consciousness comes partly from the fact that it is indeed open to alternative interpretations; but the symbol itself must be voted up or down on grounds of its symbolic appropriateness to the truth of faith.

It is easy to see why theologians should treat traditional symbols so high-handedly. Some, like "Father" meaning "God," have been used in various times and circumstances to legitimize oppression, especially of women, as the work of Rosemary Ruether and Mary Daly has made emphatically clear. Others, like "body of Christ" meaning "church," have all too often identified institutional Christianity with the Word made flesh, in an unabashedly triumphalist manner. Probably most religious symbols have similarly checkered histories; but their misuse for unworthy political and social motives is extraneous to their character as symbols. No symbol is immune to such abuse as it is culturally conditioned; but to suppose that it is nothing but a conditioned reflex of culture is a gross, gratuitous misunderstanding of its essential nature.

Theology is not ideology; its symbols are not rationalizations or justifications of any *status quo;* on the contrary, they give needed continuity and integrity to the theological enterprise itself. In his great, unheralded work titled *Herrlichkeit* the Swiss theologian von Balthasar has wisely called attention to the "aesthetic measure" proper to all doctrinal and theological statements. Theologians who know what they are about are not engaged in extracting concepts from symbols; rather, they are working to fashion and refashion symbols, pruning and refining them certainly, but not dispensing with them to get on with more important ideational business. The clarity and coherence that theologians seek is at least as much symbolic as conceptual.

The second consequence of the viewpoint sketched here for doing theological work may be noted more briefly. Present-day theology is marked by a widespread feeling of uncertainty about its future course. Into this vacuum of purpose have rushed many well-intentioned but fractured efforts to "make theology relevant" by tying it into pressing personal and social concerns. Hence we have theologies of liberation, of self-realization, of revolution, of political or racial justice, rather than theology done by a community of men and women inspired by shared visions of "the last, best hope of earth." Ethnicity and biography, ecology and typology, sexuality and ontology, are all legitimate concerns for theologians with private and public commitments; but can they afford the desperately needed perspective and orientation for theology's very survival?

It may be a healthy sign that theologians are wondering what they can do that activists or therapists cannot do better, but only if their wonderment bears fruit in sturdier and more spacious interpretations of Christian faith than most current teaching and writing indicate. The right direction for theology to take was pointed out by H. Richard Niebuhr more than a decade ago:

I look for a resymbolization of the message and the life of faith in the one God. Our old phrases are worn out; they have become clichés by means of which we can neither grasp nor communicate the reality of our existence before God. Retranslation . . . is not possible unless one has direct relations to the actualities to which people in another time referred with the aid of such symbols.[30]

This bit of prophecy in the imperative mode invites response on several counts. One comment to be made is that what Niebuhr envisaged is already taking place —and on a broadening theological front. The search for fresh images and metaphors goes on, as theologians devise new models and scenarios for understanding the transcendent in human and more-than-human terms. It is now clearer than at any time in recent memory that the theologian is a special kind of artist, a fashioner of icons and themes capable of evoking and addressing contemporary consciousness. The narrow bases of revelational positivism or systematic analysis from which we were trained to operate are giving way to larger, more pliable angles of theological vision. A loosening of worn-out categories and a rash of new proposals may be expected. The process of resymbolizing is very much in evidence.

Another comment: Niebuhr's point about "direct relations" to "actualities" is borne out by the reawakened interest in experience that characterizes theological work at present. For a generation, theologians were taught to distrust the promptings of experience, especially religious experience, as being not only irrelevant but misleading to their distinctive task of explicating the truth of Christian faith. Now, on the contrary, a turn or return to experience as the matrix of theological reflection is generally to be noted. Indeed, it could hardly be otherwise; the burgeoning of disciplines and centers for cultivating sensory awareness, expanding consciousness, and strengthening interpersonal relationships constitutes a challenge to religion that cannot go unheeded; moreover, the decided shift away from Continental influence on the part of British and North American theologians provides a real opportunity for them to be true to their own historic genius, instanced by Edwards and Bushnell, for doing truly empirical theology.

A third observation is that theology today, as Niebuhr predicted, has begun to grasp its continuity with and responsibility for its own past. Rather than trading old clichés for new ones or simply substituting currently acceptable for inacceptable interpretations of Scripture and tradition, an increasing number of theologians now see their task more in terms of a stewardship of Christian truth that calls for neither distrust of the old nor uncritical embrace of the new. Clearly what the present situation requires is a *creative fidelity* that can appreciate and appropriate the "actualities" somehow constant as well as variable in human experience and existence, to which no one style or symbol can possibly do justice but which clamor nonetheless for recognition and understanding. Liberal theologians of another era used to speak of "abiding experiences in changing categories"; with the help of anthropologists, psychologists, and sociologists we can see more clearly than before the truth in this theme; the time is ripe for recalling it into theological service. To the theologian, nothing human is alien, and the realm of transcendence symbols is the most human of all.

Our own theological situation, mutable and vulnerable as it is, nevertheless holds genuine promise for the cultural future of humankind. We theologians are not the ideologues of an ancestral faith, but neither are we available for instant use by those engaged in the arena of debate over pressing public issues and common causes. It is our mission to reintroduce our contemporaries to the standing mysteries of human life, by making them present again in symbols of transcendence capable of inspiring belief and commanding devotion. An arduous task, certainly, but also one that is both theologically authentic and humanely urgent.

4

Theologizing Transcendence

NEAR THE BEGINNING of this essay I suggested that the God question is part of the hidden agenda in discussion of transcendence, and indeed that it is bound up with our very asking of the humanity question. Meanwhile, we have been poking about in odd corners that may seem quite foreign to theology in the proper, narrow, and accepted sense—symbols, experiences, meanings, values, that range through the whole gamut of an all-too-human existence. Where does all this leave God, or rather, belief in God? It is a fair question which deserves an honest answer.

I

There are at least three major reasons for this hesitation on the part of theologians to make God the explicit subject of their work today. One reason is that religious language generally has become difficult for many people to follow, even those who gather regularly in churches and synagogues presumably to "hear a word from the Lord." The old, old story is still told and sung and listened to, of course, but there is much in our secularized world that makes it very hard to believe, at any rate for longer than one hour a week. Stouthearted fundamentalists may seem to be exceptions to this rule; but their protesting too much only proves the rule, since it betrays an agitation thinly disguised as assurance. The fact is that ways of looking at life in the world have drastically altered, leaving less and less room for what old words like creation, redemption, or sin meant to earlier generations. Other pictures have been lavishly supplied by the sciences, by literature, and by political as well as by private experience—pictures that appear to be in flat contradiction to a Biblical and Christian understanding. The idea that human history has its origin and destiny in eternity, or that the choices people make today and tomorrow have momentous meaning for their ultimate salvation, has simply become more and more of a cultural improbability.

So what line is a responsible theologian supposed to take? Mere reiteration laced with large amounts of religious nostalgia is not helpful and may even be dishonest. The question for the theologian as for every other person is that asked by the Spanish philosopher Unamuno decades ago: "Are we alone in the universe, or not?" A faith crisis is upon us all, and the sooner it is recognized by theologians the better. Hence it comes as no surprise that contemporary theology should have turned from talking about what makes God divine to talking about what makes men and women human. Here at all events some common ground can be found with the life that is given us to live. A class in theology was once addressed by John Marsh, then principal of Mansfield College, Oxford, on the topic of the Holy Spirit. Much of what he said I have forgotten, but not his concluding sentence: "The Holy Spirit comes not to make humans Christian but to make Christians human." Nothing could better illustrate the basic, enforced shift of theological direction and interest today.

This brings up the second reason for hesitating to indulge publicly in God talk: People are bound to misunderstand, since they hear such different things when the word "God" is used, depending upon their own religious backgrounds as well as upon the whole confusing weight of dimly recalled traditions. The synonyms are not of much assistance either. If we say "Father," do we intend to call up ancient ghosts of patriarchal society when fatherhood meant ownership and unquestioned authority over the family, or do we merely project onto a cosmic scale the paternalism of the good provider, the bumbling breadwinner of current television shows? And if we say "Lord," are we much better off? Hardly, since models of kingship and majesty, so appropriate before, have lost their clout with most of us in the present-day world. Thus a theologian is faced with a real dilemma: either to go on talking about God as if nothing had happened to create the risk of being misunderstood, or to develop one's own technical and rather "in-house" language which none but a few fellow professionals are going to understand anyway. It can be a somewhat painful choice.

The third reason is, I believe, the strongest and most decisive of all. It is that which we have seen coming to the surface repeatedly in this book. Transcendence, formerly regarded as the exclusive prerogative of deity, now takes in many of the wider, deeper ranges of human experience itself. It no longer can be used by theologians to mean God's total otherness from everything natural and human, to that which is beyond all time and space, unknowable and absolute and eternal. Some theologians, it is true, continue to insist on using the term in the traditional way; but meanwhile it has been turning up in secular contexts to describe the more dynamic, symbolic, self-surpassing features of an existence that is uniquely human. God the great Outsider, infinitely distant and unapproachable but always watchful, has become more a matter of doubt than a matter of faith. His name cannot now so readily be invoked to shame our ignorance and rebuke our pride, as if transcendence drew an uncrossable line of worth and being between humanity and deity.

When Søren Kierkegaard announced his highly personal discovery of "the infinite qualitative distinction" between man and God, he set in motion—after a long interval of neglect—forces that dominated Christian theology for more than an entire generation. Growing political and cultural despair, fed by experiences of personal anxiety and alienation, mightily helped to underscore this reading of human impotence and wrongness. Where had we to turn but to a wholly other God? Then, already in the time of the Second

World War, Dietrich Bonhoeffer, writing from prison, called this understanding of divine transcendence into serious moral and theological question. It was precisely his experience of disillusionment with the powers that be, his sense of frustrated vocation and community, which brought him to a new and different understanding. He came to believe that a "God of the gaps" somehow existing at the edge of things had become an impossible notion for Christians to accept. Instead, he proposed "God in the midst of life," a "this-worldly transcendence," as he put it, since "only a suffering God can help."

For Bonhoeffer, this decisive alteration of the very meaning of divine transcendence had become not only culturally and personally but *theologically* necessary. It was no mere concession to secularity but had the whole strength of the Christian gospel behind it. His theological vision, however one-sided and disruptive of Christian continuity it may have seemed to be, was actually deriving much of its substance from more ancient and universal sources. The fathers of the church, at any rate, knew nothing of a God who was pushed out to the outer margins of reality, who simply lorded it over his creation or controlled history and nature at an infinite distance. Something had happened to the primal intuition of the gospel; something needed to be set right and given theological prominence. What was at stake was nothing less than the credibility of Christian faith in God.

Dietrich Bonhoeffer would surely have been appalled to realize that present-day radical theologians employ his revised view of transcendence for the purpose of making belief in God unnecessary. Everything worth saving in the Christian understanding of God, they assert, can be preserved and restated in the language of human self-transcendence. So we now have "theologies" of liberation, of hope for the future, of process, of the body, even atheistic theologies that propose to affirm humanity by denying God. Each of them is intent on recovering a lost and needed accent within the delicate balance of Christian truth. But each protests too much, pushing its own partial truth at the expense of the whole truth. Small wonder, then, that people find all this extremely confusing rather than clarifying and ask what theology has come to.

The problem here, or at least a large part of the problem, seems to lie in the connection between time and truth. The notion that truth is a variable function of time is an appealing one, and it is confidently proclaimed in many quarters. Hitching stars to wagons rather than wagons to stars becomes the general preoccupation; relevance is believed to determine truth rather than truth determining relevance. So far as theology is concerned, this use of a pragmatic *a priori* to decide issues of truth or falsity in Christian thinking appears to be widely accepted. That which cannot be updated may be safely put aside or discarded.

Now, all theology gives evidence of the time in which it is done; it mirrors changes in the culture out of which it emerges and reveals in style as well as substance the marks of its cultural alliances and com-

mitments, even where these are not affirmed intentionally. But it does not follow from this contextual
conditioning that theology is nothing but a form of
cultural response whether critical or approving. Still
less does it follow that what conditions theological
work in a particular epoch must be taken as its goal or
conscious purpose. The fact that ours is a politicized
age does not mean that only a political theology is true
theology.

As the contours of experience change, so do the
stresses and salients in theological endeavor. A world
come of age, in Bonhoeffer's phrase, will have to get
along as best it can without God the overlord, the
terrible starer, the crutch. But what makes possible the
resolute dismissal of such ways of symbolizing God,
what renders them both untimely and unworthy, is
precisely the conviction that theology is something
more than saying yes or no to changes in its culture.
Its truth is not so easily to be manipulated or pin-
pointed, since it subtends a larger, longer arc of
meaning.

Indeed, tradition and revolution in theology are not
as far apart as one might think. Every tradition was
once a kind of revolution, just as every revolution
harks back to an older and forgotten tradition. The
truth that informs theological work is not timeless but
perennially timely. It may not all be equally "relevant"
and yet it remains available for insight and guidance,
for correcting cultural astigmatisms as for broadening
human vision of the one thing needful through the
shocks and changes of this mortal life.

II

One cannot dispose of the God question by concentrating on the humanity question. These are actually the same question, since today transcendence has become a common and not a divisive frontier. Not only theology but all the arts and sciences are engaged in reflective explorations into this zone of human being, and one hopes that conversation between these disciplines will grow and flourish. In the meantime, personal and interpersonal experiences of the transcendent are reported and recorded, often clinically, thus raising anew the universal inquiry into what makes men and women human. How may we take the *theological* measure of all these developments and researches?

Theologians of a conservative bent are likely to be put off by the very announcement of such a project. Does it not mean blurring ancient theological distinctions between finite and infinite, temporal and eternal, profane and sacred? The Protestant reformers insisted on the principle *Finitum non capax infiniti*—the finite is incapable of knowing or experiencing the infinite. Insofar as this serves notice and warning upon those who would reduce the meaning of the word "God" to cognitive manageability, it is certainly valid and deserves to be heeded. But it is sometimes made to say far more than this. "No way from man to God, only a way from God to man" was Karl Barth's early version of the principle. That, he taught a whole theological generation, is what "transcendence" means.

By removing it altogether from the natural and human realm, by locating it in God alone and then defining God as the *totaliter aliter,* or wholly other, the early Barth went classical Protestantism one better.

Oddly enough, however, this Barthian accentuation of the Reformation principle claims to know too much. What begins as a confession of human incapacity has been turned into a declaration regarding the infinitely capable God. Only the infinite can know the finite. God cannot be known unless he makes himself known, which he does in revelation. Usually we have spoken of "knowing God," but this way of speaking needs theological correction. Turning the modern subject-object format inside out, as it were, Barth's theology was predicated on the axiom that God is always the infinite Subject, man the finite object. This tour de force makes it impertinent to ask how the finite is able to know the difference between itself and the infinite, or indeed, how it knows itself to be finite at all. Such questions are even blasphemous, for they represent proud reason's effort to pry into divine mystery. Revelation alone, issuing from the absolutely other God, can surmount the human barrier of finitude.

When theology attempts to put humanity in its proper, subordinate place before God it is engaged in a strange procedure. The theo-logic of revelation seems to demand that God's right to be God must be asserted quite apart from any awareness or address-ability in the human object. But is not the test of revelation always that it *reveals*? The human being who "receives" revelation is more than merely a receiver;

he or she on Barth's own terms becomes "God's other," made more fully human by the revelatory act. Further, human finitude is no bare reflex of God's speaking out of the realm of all-transcending infinity; it is experienced, rather, as guilt, limitation, or frustration—namely, as a principle violated, a resistance encountered, or a purpose thwarted. Is this not to say that self-transcendence is bound up with every experience of being transcended? The consciousness of falling short, or being confined or alienated, cannot be understood, much less even described, without reference to some state of being that makes these ways of existing what they are experienced to be. We never experience transcending or being transcended in anything like a pure, unambiguous state; they are given together and may not be separated, however carefully they may be distinguished in speech or thought.

It is instructive at this point to notice how Barth deals with the view of Ludwig Feuerbach and his successors. Their way of reading the language of transcendence is to say that all theology is really a disguised anthropology; its statements about God should be taken as referring to humanity instead. Theology may indeed give valuable information, even insight, as to human self-understanding; but one is merely self-deceived if theology is thought to refer to anything above or beyond experience. "Man is the God of man," wrote Feuerbach; "I deny only in order to affirm. I deny the fantastic projection of religion and theology in order to affirm the real essence of man."[31]

As might be expected, theologians have generally rejected or tried to refute this unfriendly estimate of their enterprise. Perhaps, however, the vehemence of theological reaction only masks an uneasy suspicion that an affirmative truth is lurking behind Feuerbach's rhetoric of denial. What honest modern theologian has never once entertained the possibility that convictions concerning God, like the established certitudes of historic faith itself, may be nothing but probes launched into the unknown from the shaky platform of an all-too-human self-understanding? Since belief that is too sure of itself to bear criticism and correction only confesses its own lack of belief, so a theology that cannot absorb the attacks of radical doubt is but an exercise in "fantastic projection."

Barth liked to use the example of Feuerbach to frighten students and readers into seeing just where radical "subjectivism" or "empiricism" must always lead. What he found theologically intolerable here was "the possibility of an inversion of above and below, of heaven and earth, of God and man"—an overstepping of the Reformation principle *Finitum non capax infiniti.* At the same time, he could treat Feuerbach's position as "a thoroughly sound reminder, necessary for a knowledge of the real God," since it confronts the theologian with "the question of whether he is really concerned with God and not with the apotheosis of man."[32]

Present-day theologians may well have some unfinished business to do with Feuerbach. Mere refutation on the basis of a contradictory reading of the human evidence will no longer suffice. There can be no genuine or fruitful dialogue of theology with the human sciences until the anthropological character of religious assertions about God is fully accepted and explored. Both Barth and Feuerbach seem to have agreed in thinking of human experience as in principle closed rather than open, as nothing but subjective states of consciousness. On this premise what seemed affirmation to the latter was only denial to the former. When presuppositions so completely antithetical are brought to the discussion of experience, what possible community of understanding can emerge?

Today, however, as was mentioned earlier, fundamental reorientations are in process that shift "the index pointer of reality"; old dualisms have become "polarities"; the well-worn oppositions of "fact" and "value," of "experienced" and "real," of "inner" and "outer," are no longer operational in most quarters where what is uniquely human is being investigated. Meanwhile, new links are being forged, hitherto unsuspected but now looking toward more sensitive and spacious perspectives.

Let us then shift our focus in theology from a superbeing called "God" to the examination of those experiences of transcending and being transcended which give rise to religious faith and provide the only valid testing ground for its theological interpretation. The spirit of such a proposal is caught by Herbert Fingarette, who writes this about a protagonist in an ancient Hebrew drama:

Job saw finally that the divine meaning of life is to be found in the numinous and indwelling quality of life lived and accepted in all its mysterious and untamable variety, not in supposed references to superlife Entities, Doings, or Compacts nor with an eye to the earthly rewards and punishments visited upon us from such a super-human world. Job learned that the meaning of life is not something outside life upon which to lean, not something outside life to which life points.[33]

Here again the operative term is "meaning," as it was for Ernest Hocking's work. It may prove to be the common term facilitating unprecedented breakthroughs in the near future. Instead of defending the threatened territory of transcendence, theologians would then be intent upon exploring "the numinous and indwelling quality of life." This would not be, as Barth feared, an inversion of the Reformation principle, for theology has always been anthropology in that it is contexted and conditioned by relativities and profundities germane to human experience itself. "God and the soul I desire to know," wrote Augustine in his *Soliloquies.*

It is necessary to go on denying Feuerbach's denials, since one function of theology is to protest against any nothing-but account of the transcendent. Facile and overpositive reductionism of any kind is inimical to growth in understanding, and especially when it crops up in theologizing itself. Nevertheless, it is a generally sound principle that one's viewpoint is more likely to be true in what it affirms than in what it denies. Applying this to Feuerbach, Marx, Nietzsche, or

Freud as interpreters of experiential religion, it may be maintained that God, or, better, transcendence, is what human experience *means*. Of course Feuerbach never said this, but perhaps now we are able to say it for him.

A good example of the changed perspective in theology is Gregory Baum's treatment of Providence. He believes that statements once made about a superperson or "Supreme Being" called "God" can and should be read now as "a message of hope in regard to human life." There is no possible answer, he claims, to such questions as "What does God know?" or "What can God do?" They are wrongly put because they assume that information is available, through revelation and tradition, that we do not in fact possess. What we do have, however, says Father Baum, is the good news that a summons toward better insight, a strengthening to see, to do, and to be in a newer, more creative way is mysteriously present in every situation that men or women have to face. This is what used to be called the wisdom and power of God, explicated in theology by theories of omniscience and omnipotence. But today the word "God" is no longer required in order to celebrate and lay hold on "the transcendent mystery, immanent in man's making of man, by whose wisdom he enters into truth and by whose will he re-creates his life."[34]

This process of translation from divine into human terms is not as simple as it looks. In all translation there is both gain and loss of meaning; so also here. This effort to give up the outsider-God as a reference point apart from self-transcending humanity is well taken, but it does not signal the dismissal or disappearance of a whole range of meanings that do not come through this particular translation. As Karl Barth remarked, we do not say God merely by speaking of man in a loud voice; and neither do we thereby eliminate God altogether from our speaking, or at least our thinking.

Nevertheless, Father Baum's effort at translation deserves much respect. He clearly sees that belief in God has eroded to the point where different ways of saying the same thing must be used. He offers an approach that can get us off the dead center of talking interminably about God talk in theology. Although he may be a bit too sure of the power of language changes to alter actual believing, the shift of focus he exemplifies does make it possible to understand ancient texts and themes with fresh veracity and vigor.

A further instance of the new style in theology is Paul Tillich's remarkable analysis of human courage. It is to be regretted that our major theological and ethical traditions have tended to leave courage to non-Christian philosophers as a "pagan virtue," perhaps because of its association with Stoic self-sufficiency and self-control. Tillich's treatment of this neglected topic does much to correct Christian ethical vision at an important point. He affirms that "every courage to be has an open or hidden religious root" and is therefore a "key to the ground of being" since "the ultimate power of self-affirmation can only be the power of being-itself."[35] Obviously, for Tillich courage is no "merely human" act but one that requires, and receives, systematic theological interpretation. What Tillich terms "the unconditional element in human experience," or "the power of being which is effective in every act of courage," is integral to that act itself.[36]

Thus we do not get rid of all the meanings bound up in the symbol God by translating them into deliberately human language. The God question is integral to the humanity question which is being raised in our time with almost obsessive frequency. Any attempt to keep these questions separate, or to answer them in isolation from each other, is only a confession of unwillingness to grasp and to be grasped by the whole of truth to which theology must always bear witness.

III

In an essay published recently Paul van Buren asks, "Is transcendence the word we want?" Probably not, he thinks, because of its long association with the dark or yonder side of God. He takes particular exception to Gordon Kaufman's interpretation of transcendence experiences as disclosing human limitation and thereby implying an ultimate Limiter, or God. Without denying that men and women do face genuine "boundary situations" or that resisting obscurities and obstacles are encountered in experience, van Buren holds that it is wonder rather than limit that provides the needed clue. The redirecting of attention he suggests is valuable, surely, in opening up some long-neglected linkages between aesthetic and reli-

gious experiences which theologians ought to be in-
vestigating.[37]

"Transcendence" is still the word we want, provided that it includes in its purview experiences of
transcending as well as those of being transcended.
To speak more precisely, each of these kinds of experience includes the other, so that we never have either
of them in a pure or simple state. An experience of
being limited, unless it is to be dismissed as sheer
"projection," must include some sense—however dim
—of the limiting factor itself. Conversely, if my experience takes on the dominant tone of wonder, it will by
the same token also embrace the sense—perhaps
affectively minor—of real overagainstness or radical
otherness. Being transcended and transcending are
thus given together in experience. What Barth calls
"God" and Feuerbach calls "man" are not so far apart
experientially as revelational theology and atheistic humanism would have us believe.

Our concern here is with the theological interpretation of these modes of transcendence. If to be transcended is also in some real sense to transcend, what
does this mean for Christian faith in God? It does
seem that the situation in theology has changed quite
decisively. Reinhold Niebuhr built his analysis of human nature on the premise that "spirit" signifies "self-
transcendence" as expressed in knowing, choosing,
acting, interacting with the "world" of persons and
events. But he never explored deeply the dimensions
of spirit as common to both God and humanity, and
today his analysis seems somewhat clouded by the

tendency to identify self-transcendence with sin, namely, with pride and rebellion against God as necessarily bound up with any self-surpassing power in human beings as such. In Niebuhr's view, man is ruled out of order, his motives and actions are inordinate, if he does not keep his subordinate place before the all-transcending God.

But can we actually agree with such an understanding of what being human means today? Surely not. The category of sin has by no means lost its validity; but the simplistic mapping of human selfhood on which Reformation-style theology was based can no longer be used to provide an "above-and-below" model of the God-humanity convergence. Yet much recent work on transcendence, especially by Protestant theologians, still takes as axiomatic the idea that since transcendence means God, human self-transcending must be some sort of defiance or disobedience to God—as if one had to be Nietzschean or Promethean to believe with Pascal that "man is more than man," that "man infinitely surpasses man," or that "man is made for infinity."

At the opposite pole stand those theologians who now identify transcendence with self-transcendence. They announce this shift in meaning with an enthusiasm that does seem intemperate, to be sure. In the theology of hope, so called, transcendence is simply equated with the human future; it means that tomorrow will be different from today. And in the various theologies of liberation, transcendence means political or racial or sexual freedom from previous oppression. Do not all these versions currently proclaimed in fact demolish the profounder meanings of transcendence for the sake of pinning down a more obvious, operational meaning? The symbols used to give the word a needed human relevance only express the familiar marks of the "nothing-but" syndrome all over again. And that is unfortunate, even for prosecuting those important causes for which these foreshortened meanings of transcendence are invoked.

This homogenizing of transcendence is a tour de force that constricts and distorts its meaning under the pretext of clarifying it. The ambiguity essential to the term itself has been indeed removed, with the result that no theological suggestiveness or fruitfulness remains. Yet it should not be thought that nothing can be learned or gained from secular and "radical" viewpoints regarding transcendence. Simply to reassert now that transcendence belongs solely to God and not to humanity flies in the face of too much evidence to the contrary. Some form of this-worldly transcendence is here to stay, at least until its insights have been incorporated into the ongoing work of Christian theology. And that, as we say colloquially, will take a bit of doing.

Meanwhile, a new reading of our experienced humanness is taking shape which requires theological assessment and response. One way of expressing it is to say that it concerns what is uniquely and generically human. In the contemporary arts such a concern is particularly noticeable; when artists are willing to speak about their work, they declare with astonishing frequency and vigor that it intends to probe and body forth what being human means. And in the sciences, as older naturalistic, reductionistic models are replaced by ampler and more complicated paradigms with psychic and social overtones, a similar movement of thought is being registered. Here as in the arts self-transcendence is affirmed as intrinsic to human character and growth, the dynamic ingredient uniquely present in a being who lives "forever on the verge . . . enveloped by more than is evident," so that "reality includes surprising corridors of worth that elude ordinary eyes," in the words of Huston Smith.[38]

"Transcendence" is and has to be an open-ended word, connoting both experiences of expansive, self-surpassing character and those of limiting or intrusive impact. This ambiguity in meaning is not only unavoidable but fortunate. The term can no longer be used to distinguish an entity called "man" from a superior entity called "God." In any case, language must not be taken to legislate reality questions, thus violating the Thomist principle that to distinguish is not to separate. At the same time, however, the transcendence experiences of "a self that touches all edges" (Wallace Stevens) do invite interpretation in more than solipsistic or subjective terms. They may even be said to require such interpretation.

It is also fortunate that our theological traditions in the West contain significant resources for carrying this work forward. Especially pertinent is the classical Christian understanding that God is both transcendent and immanent. The meanings of these terms are neither antithetical nor mutually exclusive; on the contrary, they are complementary and interdependent. I cannot think of immanence without also thinking of transcendence; for if one thing is said to reside or remain in another, by the same token it is said to be distinguishable from that other. Nor can I think of transcendence without also thinking of immanence; for any instance of radical dissimilarity or otherness must of course be recognized, must announce its presence, so to speak, with the ring of experienced truth.

It can scarcely be denied that such a balance as strict logic demands is difficult to strike. The linear and propositional nature of most theological language militates against this. Since it is necessary to speak or write only of one thing at a time, a certain patience and persistence are required to keep one's whole thought actively at work. "The disease of philosophy," wrote Whitehead, "is the itch to express everything in the form, All S is P, no S is P." This holds for theology as well. Nevertheless, it is the continuing task of theology to state the immanence of the transcendent without equating immanence with simple actuality, and to state the transcendence of the immanent without supposing that transcendence merely eludes or exceeds real experience.

Indeed, this is the business of theology because it is the central conviction of Christian faith. The very meaning of the gospel is that the God who was afar off has now drawn near, made our flesh his home, given himself to us through Christ our Lord. That this is no temporary visitation, no isolated event, is made clear by the doctrine of the Holy Spirit, God within us as our Enlightener, Enabler, and Enlivener. The good news for humanity is therefore also good news about humanity; since the dayspring from on high has come to dwell with us, human spirit is indwelt by Holy Spirit, freeing us to become what in the sight of God we truly are.

The reach of such faith always exceeds the grasp of theology, to be sure; yet theology's persistent search for sharable and statable meanings, though it falls short of faith, is indispensable to the furthering of faith. The case for theology can be put even more strongly. Faith itself seeks understanding, as Augustine and Anselm taught us long ago, so that theology may rightly be defined as an inquiry begun, continued, and ended in faith—a grasping of what we are grasped by, a comprehending of that which comprehends us. Such an inquiry, just because it is never finished, must forever be taken up afresh.

Present-day theology is often said to be in utter disarray, uncertain of its goals and methods, not even sure of its own subject matter. But this confusion may indicate creative ferment in response to new occasions and duties, not merely a failure of nerve. It is true that we have reached a turning point from which there can be no retreat into dogmatic security, but we must not get caught on dead center either. Now that the whole humanity-God question looms before us, baffling in its complexity and requiring fundamental reorientations in both style and substance, theologians may expect to be confused. Nevertheless as von Balthasar has written, "Humanism within Christianity is indeed the central theme of our time."[39] While this does not mean abandoning God as the subject of theological reflection, it will also involve wider explorations and more penetrating evaluations of uniquely human reality from the vantage point provided by our Christian faith.

IV

The stirrings in theology toward this changed perspective on transcendence are unmistakable today. Perhaps they are most highly visible among Roman Catholic writers and teachers, who exhibit in their work the benefits of a newly won theological freedom. Protestant theology of the most fundamental sort, as distinct from pamphleteering and special pleading which are all too prevalent, is still evidently much inhibited by the Reformation principle *Finitum non capax infiniti.* Hence there is more help to be gained in relocating transcendence from theologians like Karl Rahner, Bernard Lonergan, or Hans Urs von Balthasar, all of whom are making significant contributions in this direction. They speak out of a richer, more authentic tradition shaped in antiquity but far more pliable for present purposes than that buttressed by modern models of authority and sovereignty, or by pre-Christian symbols of patriarchal absolutism. Their allegiance is to a principle both newer and older: *Homo capax Dei,* humanity capable of God. It was probably expressed most emphatically, outside the Bible, by

Gregory of Nyssa's statement that God became what we are in order to make us what God himself is.

It cannot be a question simply of recovering this lost accent from the ancient Christian East for the sake of placing it upon the current theological agenda in the West. Yet it is heartening to realize that resources and guidelines do exist within our common heritage for carrying on our present task. Considering the antihumanism that engulfs the world on every side, theologians will need all the help they can get. There is cause for gratitude in recognizing that such help is available.

Of the Christian thinkers in our century, Nicolas Berdyaev was best able to exemplify this much-neglected perspective on divine-human transcendence. It is possible that his work now seems to have been weakened for us by a certain aristocratic disdain for massive social changes, as well as by his deep distaste for newer forms of artistic expression in his time. Yet Berdyaev could, and did, understand in a most inward way the misery of modern humans without God, believing with all his heart and mind that it would only be cured by reawakened faith in the God who became man so that man might become capable of God. He quoted Franz Baader's aphorism that although man wanted to be man without God, God did not want to be God without man, and so He became man. Believing that God-manhood was the only answer to Godforsakenness, he wrote that "Where there is no God there is no man. . . . Man without God is no longer man."[40]

The clue to be picked up from the thought of Berdyaev is that human self-transcendence may rightly be regarded as God's immanent activity as Spirit. Freedom and creativity are the very proof of our humanness, signifying participation in the energies and purposes of God. Even such language may be misleading if it gives credence to an externalizing and objectifying of what the word "God" means, so rendering it finally meaningless. Berdyaev endeavored to displace the idea of an exclusive divine transcendence with that of an inclusive divine-human transcendence. He could take fully into account the criticisms of Christianity offered by Feuerbach, Marx, Nietzsche, and Freud because he too believed that religious or theological symbols are projections of human experience rather than reports of goings-on behind and beyond the human barrier. It is in self-transcending humanity—that is, in experiencing fulfillment rather than deficiency or deprivation—that the symbols for God arise and are confirmed. Berdyaev understood well Pascal's theme of the greatness of man with God.

At present we are probably less sure than was Berdyaev of the propriety of speaking about God in objective, transexperiential terms. Not only has the logical analysis of religious language raised the question of its referential validity; still more serious is the charge, now often made, that such language is suspect because it is riddled with sexist and racist connotations. But can we not accept Berdyaev's conclusion that the word "God" has much to say regarding the meaning of humanity itself? Without it, we of the Christian West cannot begin to understand the *spiritual* character of self-transcendence. We would be reduced to a "humanism" that has even ceased to be humane.

From classical theology there are abundant resources for undertaking this new task. One is the symbol of "the image of God": humanity is said not merely to resemble God in some respects but to be capable of making visible what Karl Rahner speaks of as "the experiential mystery at the heart of human existence."[41] This capacity belongs to human beings as such, not to any single aspect or function like will or reason. What being human *means* is that we are created to be creative, thus realizing our true nature as *capax Dei*. In Berdyaev's words:

There exists a spiritual experience of the transcendent and of transcending in man. This it is impossible to deny without violence to the reality of experience. Man is a creature who transcends himself, who goes out beyond his own limits, and has eager aspiration to mystery and infinity. But the experience of the transcendent and of transcending is an inward spiritual experience, and in this sense it may be called immanent. And here by immanence is meant not rest within its own boundaries but a going-out beyond those boundaries. The transcendent reaches man not from without but from within, out of the depths. God is more deeply within me than I am myself. . . . I must transcend to my very self. The deep may be concealed in man, and this deep requires a breakthrough, a transcending.[42]

Although Berdyaev is not speaking here specifically of the *imago Dei* doctrine, his thought gives poised and positive meaning to the doctrine. His chief interest lies in making clear the spiritual, self-transcending character of human experience, traditionally expressed in image-of-God terms.

That human being is created in the image of God has traditionally been part of the doctrine of creation. There are still some theologians who employ the idea of divine creation to underscore the absolute transcendence of a primordial Creator. Yet surely it is one of the ironies of history that human creativeness should have served as the dominant image for understanding God's relation to the world, but in such a way that it only heightens and hardens the distance between the world and God. The effect has been that of minimizing or denying outright the reality of self-transcending creativity in human life, except to view it as defiance of the creator-God. Clearly, something has been going wrong here for a long time. Has the analogy from creativity been taken too seriously or not seriously enough? At all events it seems to have reversed itself; and thinkers like Berdyaev are engaged in reversing that reversal.

Another resource stemming from theological tradition may be found in the doctrine of grace. No doctrine has been more disputed, whether by Pelagians and Augustinians, Jesuits and Jansenists, or Arminians and Calvinists. Yet the churches persist in teaching and preaching grace, and Christian people persist in believing it, despite the seemingly endless controversies occasioned by it. There must be some good reason for this. Could it be that Christian experience outruns and outlasts its doctrinal formulation, so that new symbols become necessary for sharing this experience? Just this would seem to be the case. Theology then comes into its own as critical and constructive reflection on experiences of grace, informing and energizing human feeling and acting in surprising, self-fulfilling ways.

The word "grace" opens up a whole spectrum of meanings, suggested by other words like "gracefulness," "graciousness," and "gratefulness." Undoubtedly the term has always evoked the sense of unearned favor, of unexpected pleasure. The root metaphor seems to be that of bending or stooping from a higher to a lower plane. In its original meaning "condescension" well expressed this movement; as applied to God, it symbolized the right of the sovereign to do as he pleased with what is his, the gratuitousness of an absolute and unaccountable will. At the same time, however, the word "grace" cannot be understood without the complementary aspect of a gracious disposition on the part of God toward what belongs to him —a "good pleasure" that seeks and effects the well-being and indeed the happiness of those who call themselves his creatures. A large part of the holding power of the doctrine of grace in Christian theology, certainly, came from this juxtaposing of the gracious and the gratuitous within the condescending action of God. He does what he does not have to do, what humans have no right to expect from him, for our own final good and for his everlasting glory.

There is, however, a further meaning of grace that is even more important for understanding the feel of Christian experience. "Once I was blind, but now I can see"—grateful testimonies like this are the essence of grace experience. What is being described here is not merely something that happens to a person but that also takes place within the person. Grace always means the greatening of the self, an inward empowering, a being-made-new, or it is not grace that is meant. It is an experience of becoming "filled with all the fulness of God," in Paul's words, or as we might say today, of participating in the life of God. Such an experience, before it can be a springboard for theological reflection, must be tasted and shared at the level of feeling, if only by means of an imagined identity. Affectively, the tone of grace experience may be conveyed by Charles Péguy's "Grace is insidious—it twists and turns and is full of surprises," or by Simone Weil's "Grace makes us fall *toward* the heights."

Grace is *par excellence* the experience of an incoming and uplifting transcendence. But it might just as truly be termed the experience of an indwelling and en-abling immanence. Theologians have spoken of the paradox of grace as indicated by the "I, yet not I" of Paul; and yet is it really so paradoxical, except perhaps when verbalized and conceptualized? Every lover has a taste, or foretaste, of a not dissimilar experience. It is not that one's proper self is displaced or taken over by another self, but rather that "two hearts beat as one" in a common rhythm of yearning and expectancy. Whatever else grace may be said to be, it means a unitive experience in which the divine-human barrier is broken through in newness of life.

It may be too much to hope that the interminable

theological debates over grace versus free will, grace versus nature, will soon be at an end. Nevertheless, it is reasonable to think that theologians may become less obsessed with distinguishing the "I" from the "not I" and more intrigued by the possibility that human transcendence and divine immanence are given together in experiences of grace, both classic and contemporary. Paradoxical or not, that possible interpretation commends itself to theologians who are now convinced that the search for God begins with humanity's search for its own unique reality, starting out from "the self that is more at home in the infinite than here among Things," in Hocking's prophetic phrase.

A third and still largely unexplored resource for a theology of creative transcendence lies at hand in the ancient doctrine of the spirit. The work already done needs to be brought into closer touch with nontheological approaches; it would be astonishing indeed if the word "spirit" did not find its way into this burgeoning community of inquiry into what makes human beings truly and indubitably human.

True, this traditional key word has lost much of its earlier warmth and vigor in Christian usage. It has become but a nostalgic, anemic echo of its former self. Its connotations seem largely negative; most often it refers to a sequestered and shadowy form of human existing, less real by far than any sensuous, active, or social modes. Thus a "spiritual" preacher is one who avoids controversial issues, and "spiritual formation" means nurturing a privatistic, otherworldly self-awareness. The virtual disembodiment of spirit in conventional religion has of course been challenged by the charismatic and Pentecostal movements, where "spirit" denotes an intense and often ecstatic experience, as it did in apostolic times. But the theological measure of these movements, as of many other evidences of transcendence-seeking today, has yet to be taken.

At all events, the word "spirit" has not lost all its authentic meaning as the Biblical and Christian designation of a reality at once human and divine; it remains available for interpreting the sense of being open to and entered by transcendence. Like "grace," "spirit" is an oddly nonpersonal term that nonetheless sounds the depths of personal and interpersonal existence. It is and always has been faith's way of saying that "man is more than man" because our nature is to become more, to possess what we are possessed by, to seek our own transformation by means of the possibilities that define our very actuality. We are spirit insofar as our being is constituted by becoming; and becoming lies within the energizing scope of transcendence.

All this may seem excessively abstract, and yet we need nothing in present-day theology so much as spacious, nonspecific symbols for rendering the felt wholeness of what being human means. Among the best of these are the symbols that body forth the Spirit of love and truth set loose in the world through Jesus whom faith calls the Christ. That Spirit witnesses with our spirits that we are the children of God. To those

who first said this, it meant that human spirit participates in Holy Spirit, that the wall of partition between
God and man is broken down, and that because Christ
lives we may live also. Must we not still believe this?

Our ancestors in the faith spoke of the creator-
Spirit, whom they invoked in hymns like *Veni Creator
Spiritus*. Even in the beginning, God went out from
himself, stirring the primeval waters by the *ruach Elo-
him*, the breath or wind of an all-transcending purpose. Not less awesome is the kind of transcendence
that lives in human creativity itself. To bear and to be
borne by this creative transcendence is, as Henry Wie-
man has said, the zest and glory of our all-too-human,
more-than-human life. For we too are spirit, open toward infinity despite our finitude, and so moved and
shaped by the beyond that is within and among us.

Our time of unparalleled human crisis harbors the
possibility of rediscovering these liberating truths of
Christian faith. Transcendence, even if its right name
should turn out to be God, has nothing to fear from
self-transcendence. Ambiguous it surely is, fraught
with potentialities both terrifying and encouraging;
but these can be recognized and dealt with quite apart
from supposing that they violate some preestablished
boundary or other. A theology of creative transcendence will have no new lines to draw between God and
man; that will be the least of its concerns. But it will
risk and spend itself in exploring ancient meanings of
grace and the Spirit from the home base of the mystery
of being human, convinced that men and women without a past can have no real future.

Notes

1. G. L. Prestige, *God in Patristic Thought* (London: S.P.C.K., 1956), pp. 4–5, 26.

2. Nicolas Berdyaev, *The Meaning of the Creative Act* (Charles Scribner's Sons, 1955), p. 16.

3. *Ibid.*, p. 100.

4. William Ernest Hocking, *The Meaning of God in Human Experience* (Yale University Press, 1912), pp. 327, 328–329.

5. G. H. Woods, "The Idea of the Transcendent," *Soundings*, ed. by Alec Vidler (Cambridge University Press, 1962), p. 48.

6. See John E. Smith, *Experience and God* (Oxford University Press, 1968), esp. pp. 36–41.

7. Thomas Merton, *The Seven Story Mountain* (Harcourt Brace and Company, Inc., 1948), pp. 202–203.

8. Herbert Read, *Icon and Idea* (Harvard University Press, 1955), p. 140.

9. Erich Neumann, *Art and the Creative Unconscious* (Bollingen Series LXI, 1959), pp. 190, 192.

10. William S. Merwin, *Animae* (Kayak Books, 1969), pp. 22, 23.

11. Quoted in Quentin Bell, *Virginia Woolf* (Harcourt, Brace Jovanovich, 1972), Vol. I, p. 138.

12. F. David Martin, *Art and the Religious Experience* (Bucknell University Press, 1972).

13. Amos Wilder, *Grace Confounding* (Fortress Press, 1972), p. ix.

14. Gerardus Van der Leeuw, *Sacred and Profane Beauty: The Holy in Art* (Holt, Rinehart & Winston, Inc., 1963), pp. 332, 334.

15. Jacques Maritain, *Creative Intuition in Art and Poetry* (Pantheon Books, 1953), p. 9.

16. G. H. Woods, see the essay already referred to in *Soundings*, ed. by Alec Vidler (Cambridge University Press, 1962), p. 56.

17. Gabriel Marcel, *The Philosophy of Existence*, tr. by Manya Harari (Philosophical Library, 1948), pp. 25–26.

18. I owe this citation to the late Carl Michalson, who used it in his Birks Lectures at McGill University in 1964.

19. Quoted from Alan W. Watts in Philip Wheelwright, *Metaphor and Reality* (Indiana University Press, 1962), pp. 155–156.

20. Marc Oraison, *Chance and Life*, tr. by Bernard Murchland (Doubleday & Company, Inc., 1972), p. 98.

21. Dorothy Sayers, *Introductory Papers on Dante* (Harper & Brothers, 1954), p. 8.

22. Paul Ricoeur, *The Symbolism of Evil* (Harper & Row, Publishers, Inc., 1967), p. 15.

23. See, e.g., Michael Polanyi's article, "Life's Irreducible Structure," in *Science*, Vol. 160, p. 1312.

24. See B. F. Skinner, *Beyond Freedom and Dignity* (Alfred A. Knopf, Inc., 1971), pp. 205–208.

25. Benjamin Lee Whorf, *Language, Thought, and Reality* (M.I.T. Press, 1956), p. 249.

26. Hans Urs von Balthasar, *Word and Revelation, Essays in Theology I* (Herder & Herder, Inc., 1964), p. 106.

27. Isaac Penington, quoted in Sayers, *op. cit.*, p. 20.

28. John Macquarrie, *Principles of Christian Theology* (Charles Scribner's Sons, 1966), pp. 122, 120.

29. *Ibid.*, pp. 124, 125.

30. H. Richard Niebuhr, in *How My Mind Has Changed*, ed. by Harold E. Fey (Meridian Books, Inc., 1961), pp. 79–80.

31. Ludwig Feuerbach, cited in Karl Barth's introductory essay to Feuerbach, *The Essence of Christianity* (Harper & Brothers, 1957), p. xviii.

32. *Ibid.*, p. xxiii.

33. Herbert Fingarette, *The Self in Transformation* (Basic Books, Inc., 1963), p. 281.

34. Gregory Baum, *Man Becoming* (Herder & Herder, Inc., 1971), p. 242–244.

35. Paul Tillich, *The Courage to Be* (Yale University Press, 1952), pp. 156, 166.

36. *Ibid.*, pp. 170, 172.

37. Paul van Buren, "Theology Now?" *The Christian Century*, May 29, 1974, pp. 585–589.

38. Huston Smith, *Transcendence*, ed. by Herbert Richardson and Donald Outler (Beacon Press, Inc., 1969), pp. 1, 16.

39. Von Balthasar, *op. cit.*, p. 89.

40. Nicolas Berdyaev, *The End of Our Time* (Sheed & Ward, 1933), pp. 80, 54.

41. See John Carmody, S.J., "Karl Rahner: Theology of the Spiritual Life," in *New Theology*, No. 7 (The Macmillan Company, 1970), p. 110.

42. Berdyaev, *The Divine and the Human* (London: Geoffrey Bles, 1949), pp. 45–46.

32 401